STAR WARS®

THE CLONE WARS™

THE STARCRUSHER TRAP

SCRIPT **MIKE W. BARR**   ART **THE FILLBACH BROTHERS**

COLORS **RAYMUND LEE**   LETTERING **MICHAEL HEISLER**

COVER ART **THE FILLBACH BROTHERS WITH DAN JACKSON**

DARK HORSE BOOKS®

THE RISE OF THE EMPIRE
1000–0 YEARS BEFORE *STAR WARS: A NEW HOPE*

The events in these stories take place approximately twenty-two years before the Battle of Yavin.

After the seeming final defeat of the Sith, the Republic enters a state of complacency. In the waning years of the Republic, the Senate is rife with corruption, and the ambitious Senator Palpatine has himself elected Supreme Chancellor. This is the era of the prequel trilogy.

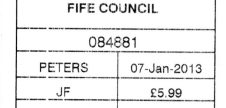

FIFE COUNCIL	
084881	
PETERS	07-Jan-2013
JF	£5.99
JCAR	FIFE

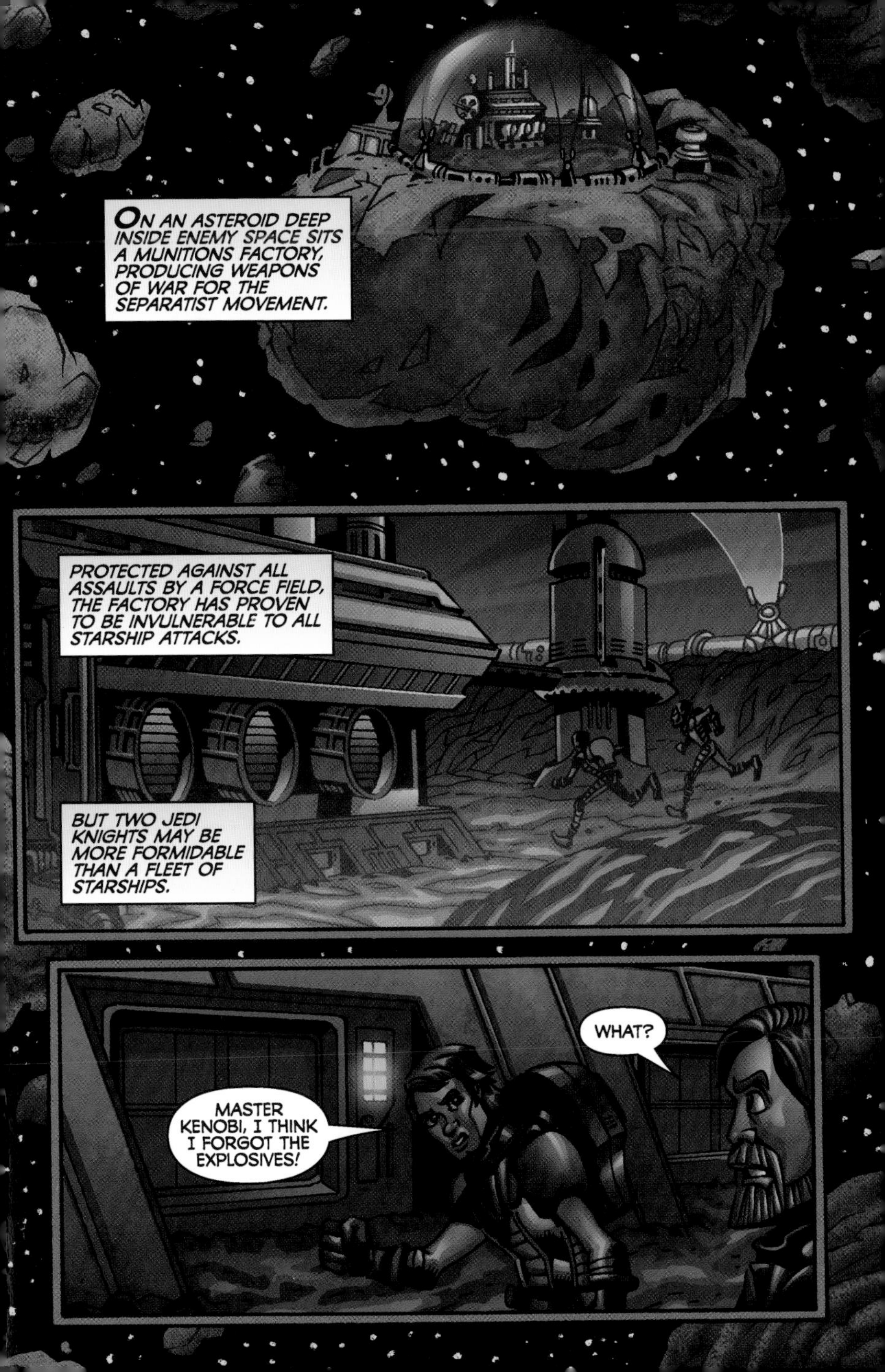
ON AN ASTEROID DEEP INSIDE ENEMY SPACE SITS A MUNITIONS FACTORY, PRODUCING WEAPONS OF WAR FOR THE SEPARATIST MOVEMENT.
PROTECTED AGAINST ALL ASSAULTS BY A FORCE FIELD, THE FACTORY HAS PROVEN TO BE INVULNERABLE TO ALL STARSHIP ATTACKS.
BUT TWO JEDI KNIGHTS MAY BE MORE FORMIDABLE THAN A FLEET OF STARSHIPS.
MASTER KENOBI, I THINK I FORGOT THE EXPLOSIVES!
WHAT?

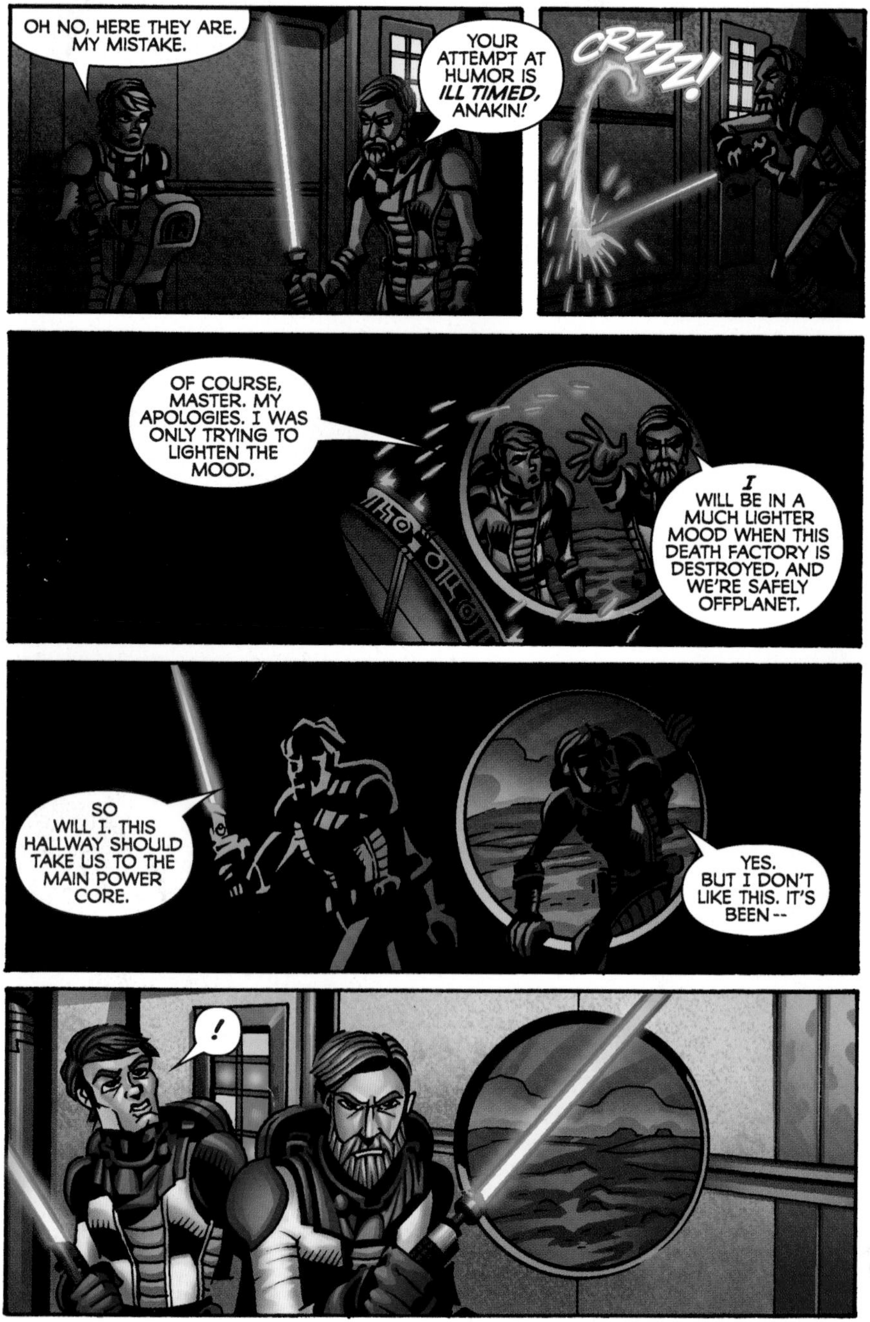
OH NO, HERE THEY ARE. MY MISTAKE.
YOUR ATTEMPT AT HUMOR IS *ILL TIMED,* ANAKIN!
CRZZZZ!
OF COURSE, MASTER. MY APOLOGIES. I WAS ONLY TRYING TO LIGHTEN THE MOOD.
I WILL BE IN A MUCH LIGHTER MOOD WHEN THIS DEATH FACTORY IS DESTROYED, AND WE'RE SAFELY OFFPLANET.
SO WILL I. THIS HALLWAY SHOULD TAKE US TO THE MAIN POWER CORE.
YES. BUT I DON'T LIKE THIS. IT'S BEEN --
!

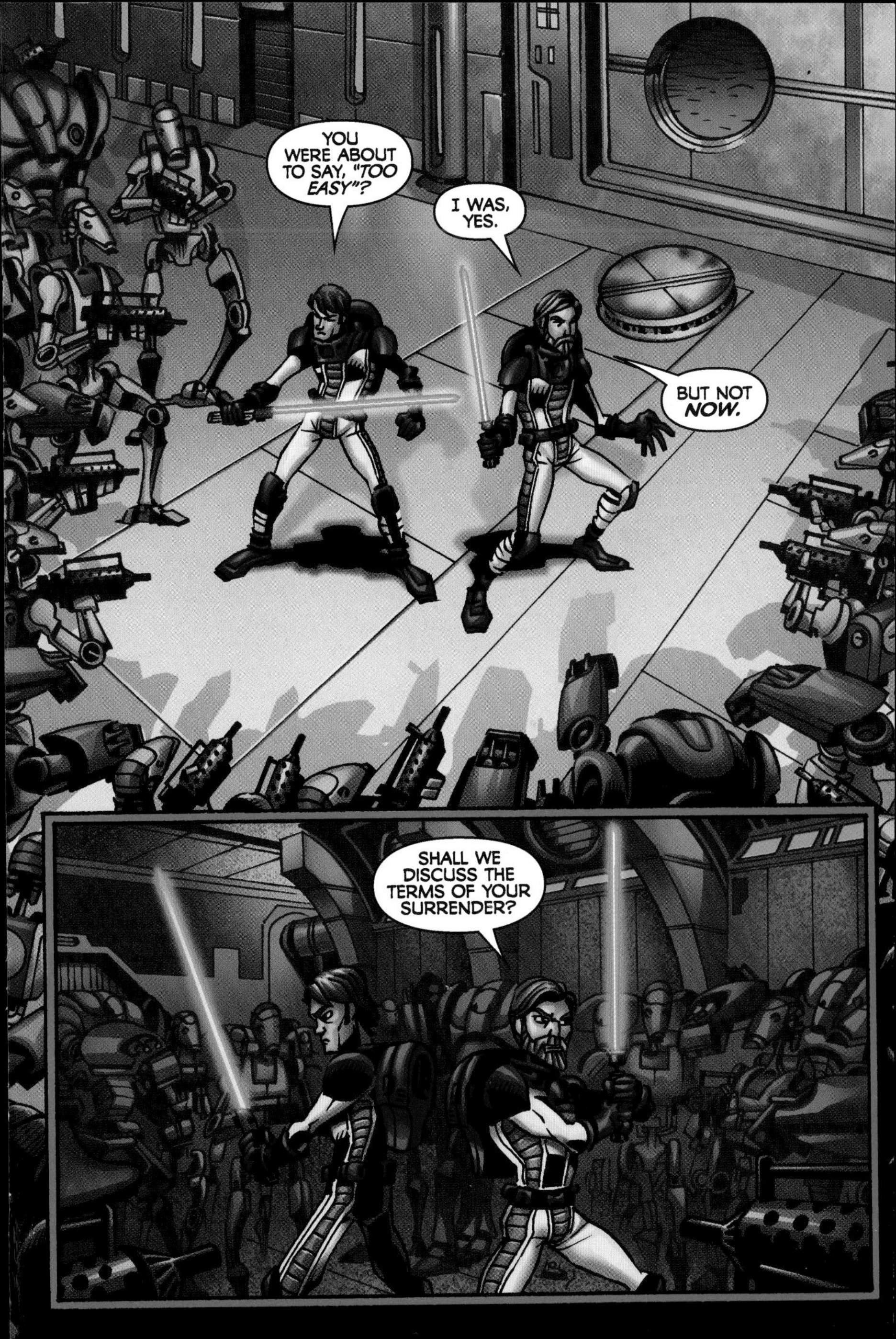
YOU WERE ABOUT TO SAY, "*TOO EASY*"?
I WAS, YES.
BUT NOT ***NOW.***
SHALL WE DISCUSS THE TERMS OF YOUR SURRENDER?

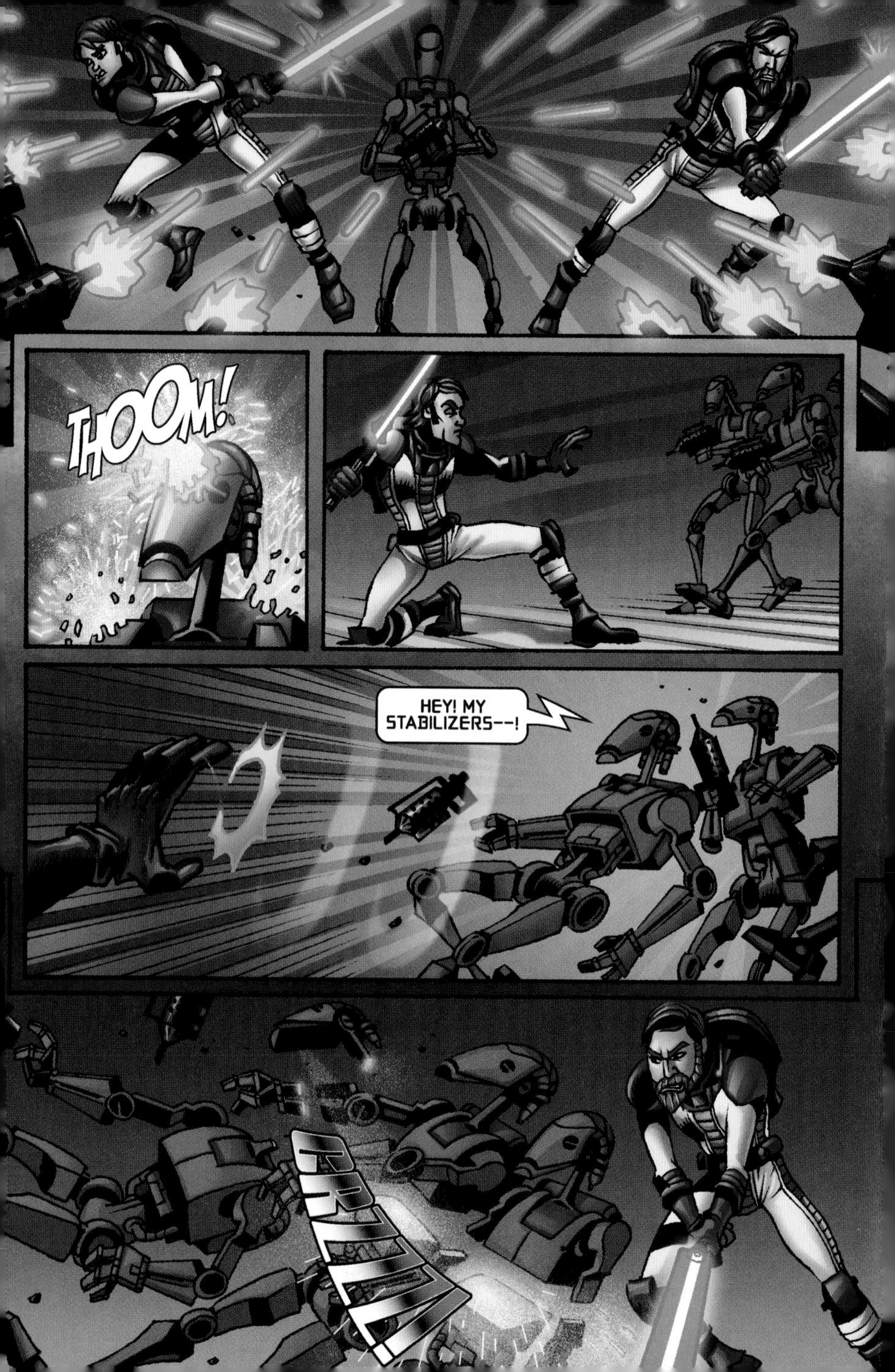
THOOM!
HEY! MY STABILIZERS--!

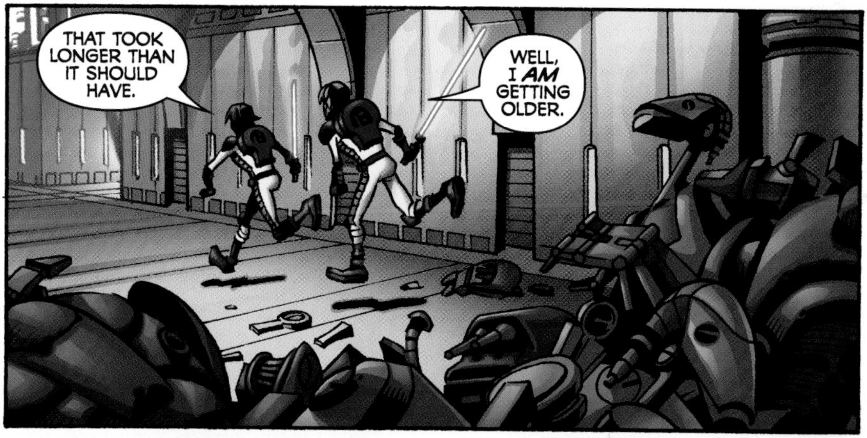
THAT TOOK LONGER THAN IT SHOULD HAVE.
WELL, I *AM* GETTING OLDER.

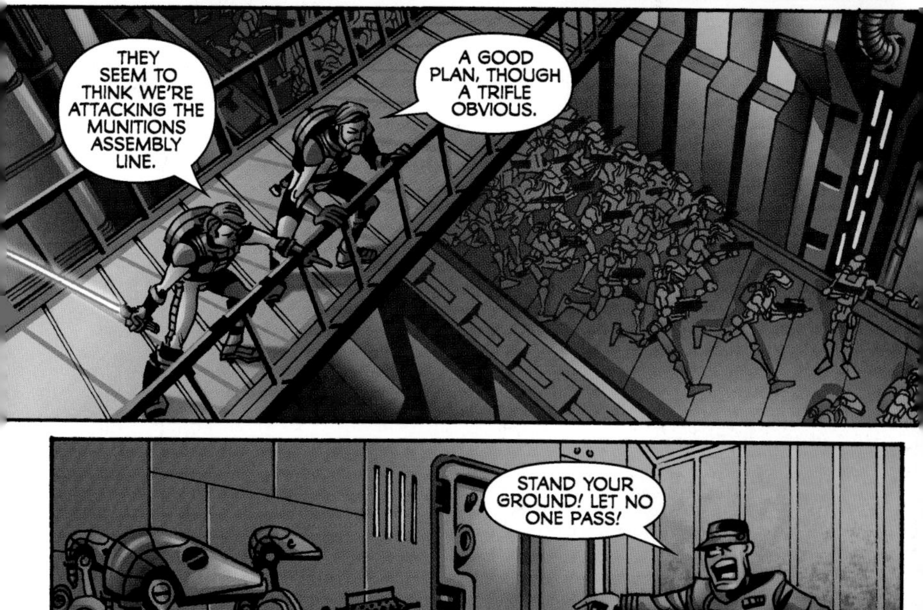
THEY SEEM TO THINK WE'RE ATTACKING THE MUNITIONS ASSEMBLY LINE.
A GOOD PLAN, THOUGH A TRIFLE OBVIOUS.

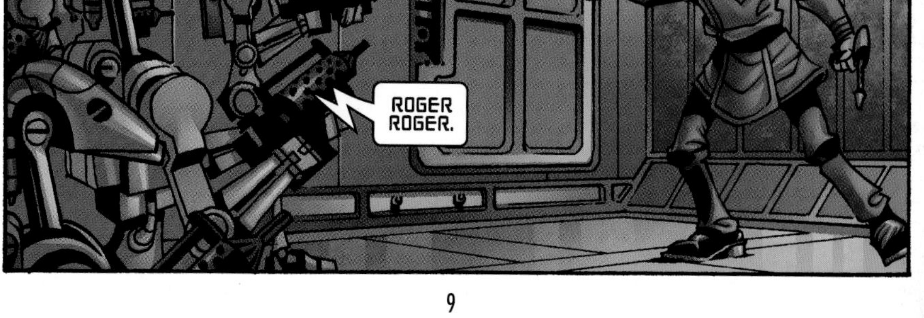
STAND YOUR GROUND! LET NO ONE PASS!
ROGER ROGER.

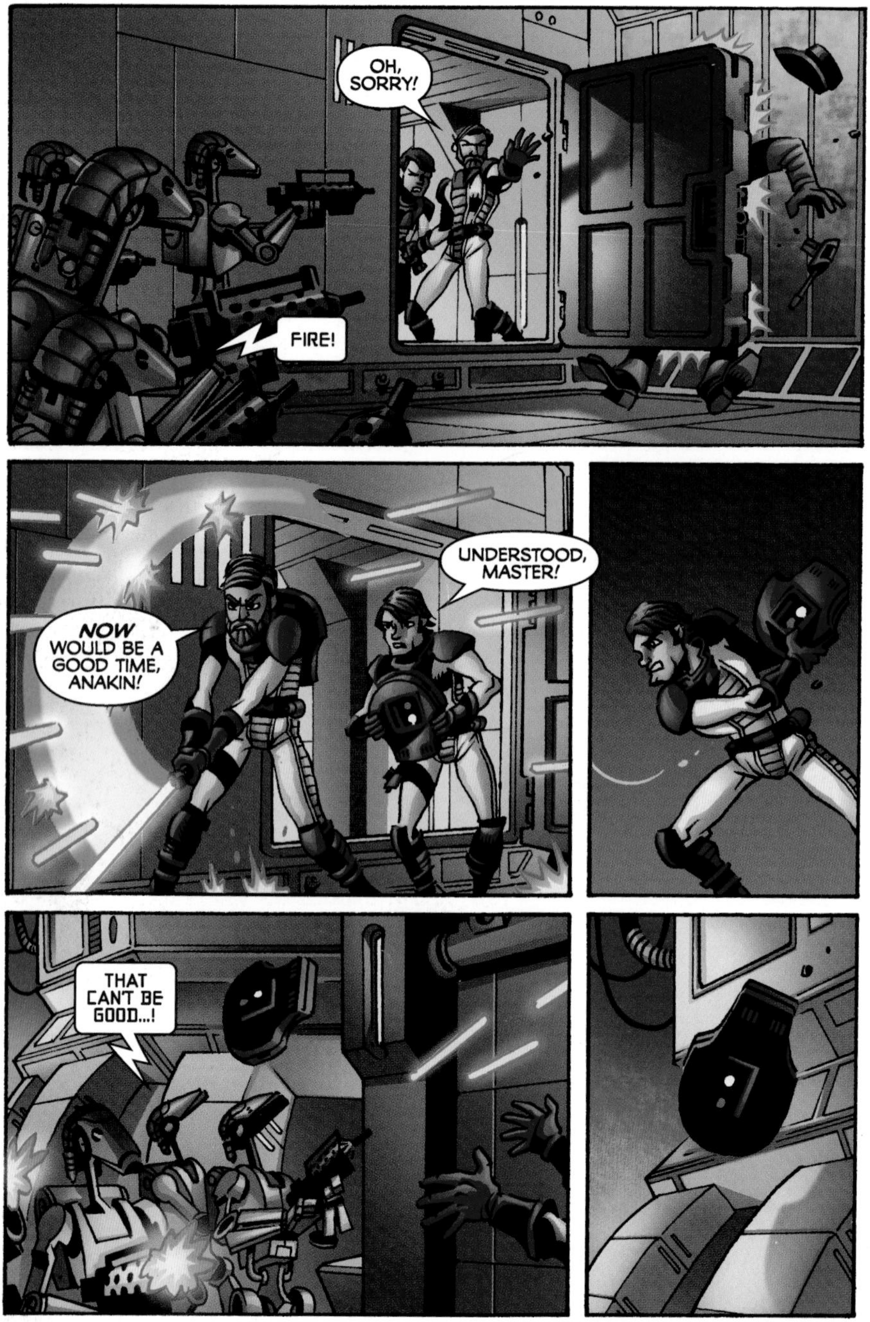
OH, SORRY!
FIRE!
NOW WOULD BE A GOOD TIME, ANAKIN!
UNDERSTOOD, MASTER!
THAT CAN'T BE GOOD...!

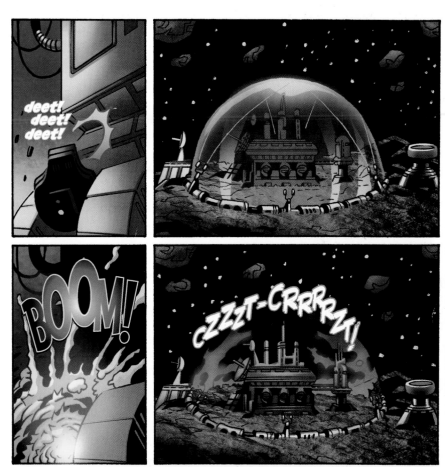

deet!
deet!
deet!

BOOM!

cZZZT-CRRRZt!

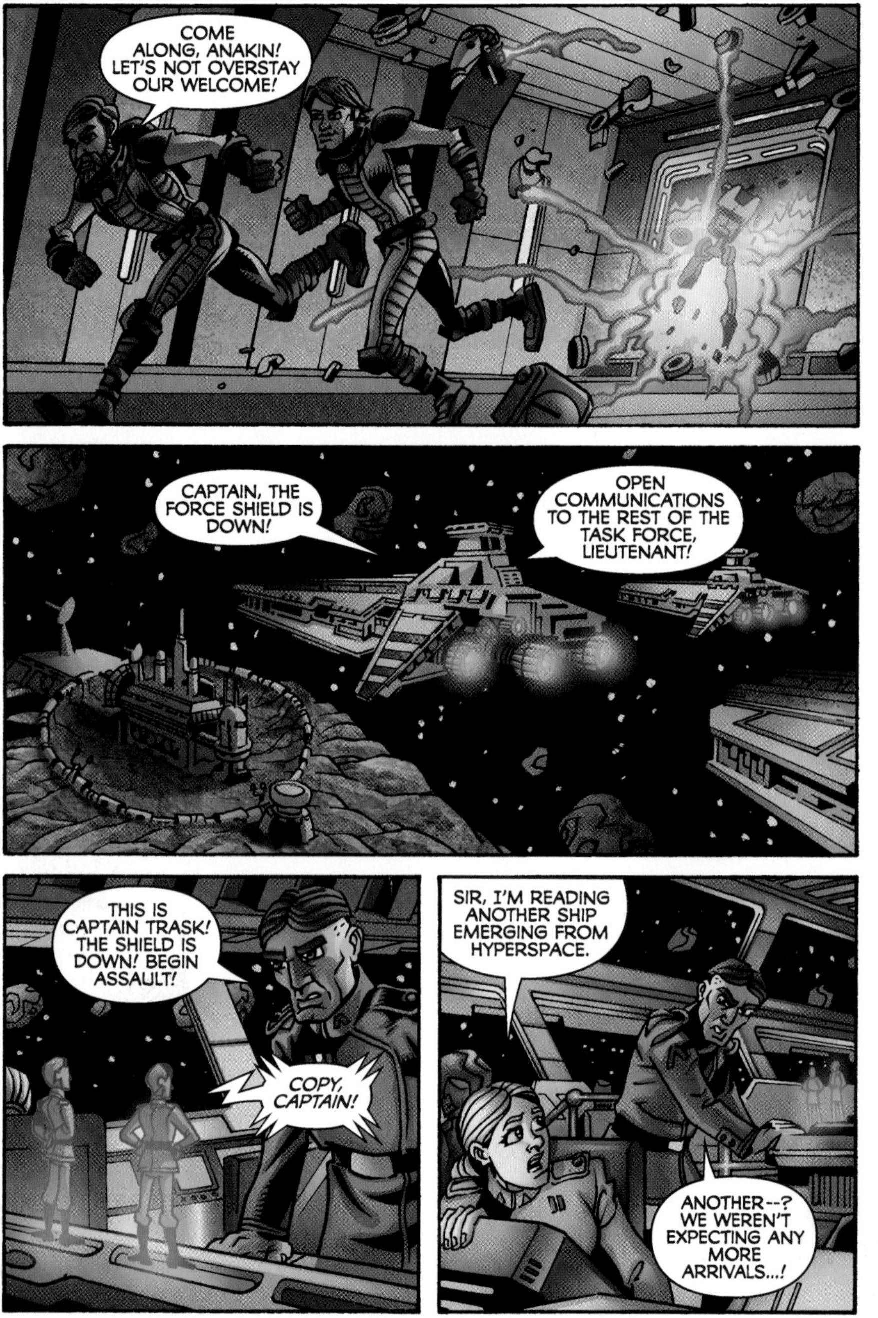
COME ALONG, ANAKIN! LET'S NOT OVERSTAY OUR WELCOME!
CAPTAIN, THE FORCE SHIELD IS DOWN!
OPEN COMMUNICATIONS TO THE REST OF THE TASK FORCE, LIEUTENANT!
THIS IS CAPTAIN TRASK! THE SHIELD IS DOWN! BEGIN ASSAULT!
COPY, CAPTAIN!
SIR, I'M READING ANOTHER SHIP EMERGING FROM HYPERSPACE.
ANOTHER--? WE WEREN'T EXPECTING ANY MORE ARRIVALS...!

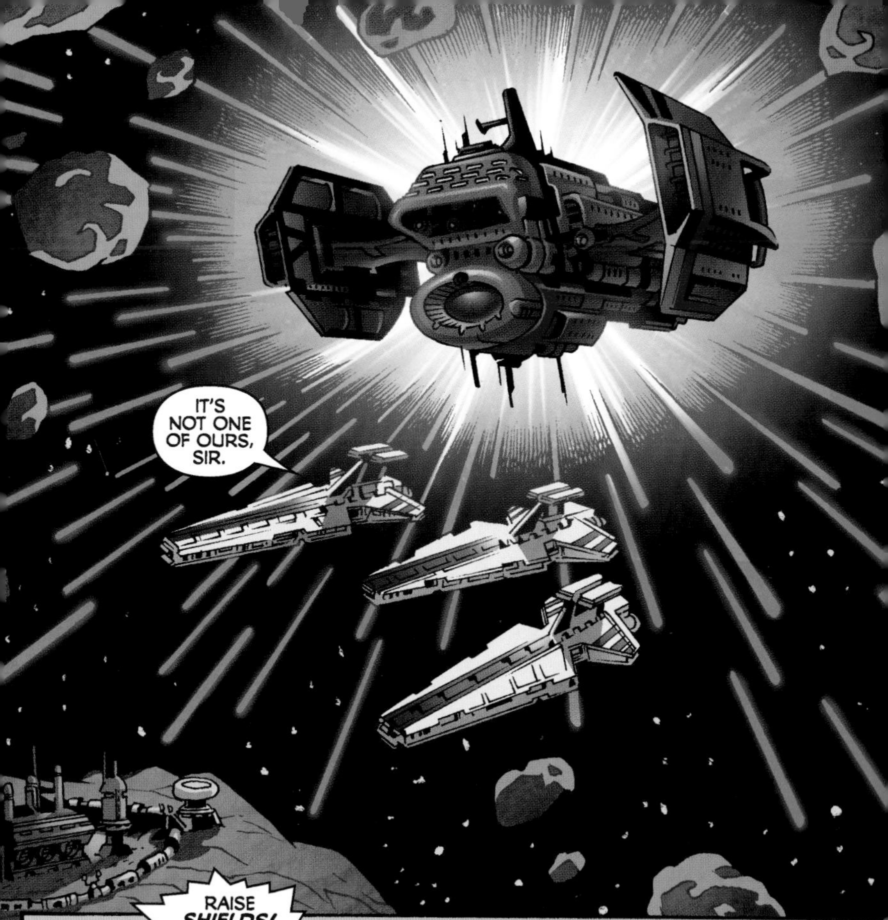
IT'S NOT ONE OF OURS, SIR.

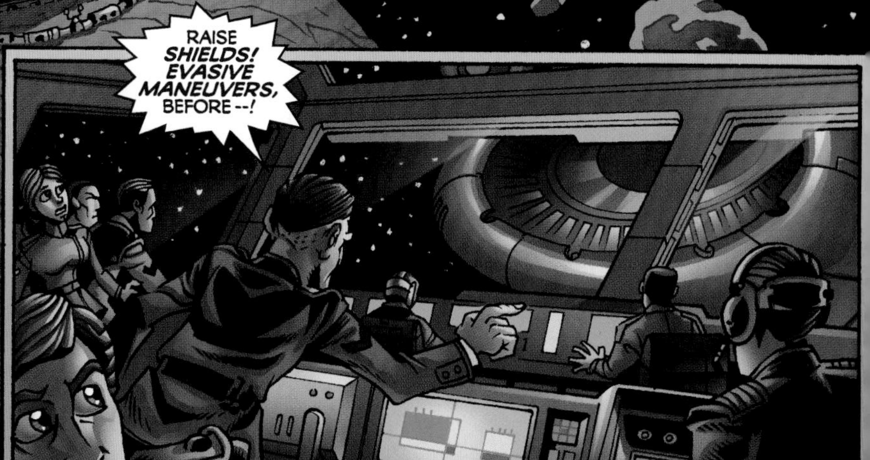
RAISE ***SHIELDS! EVASIVE MANEUVERS,*** BEFORE --!

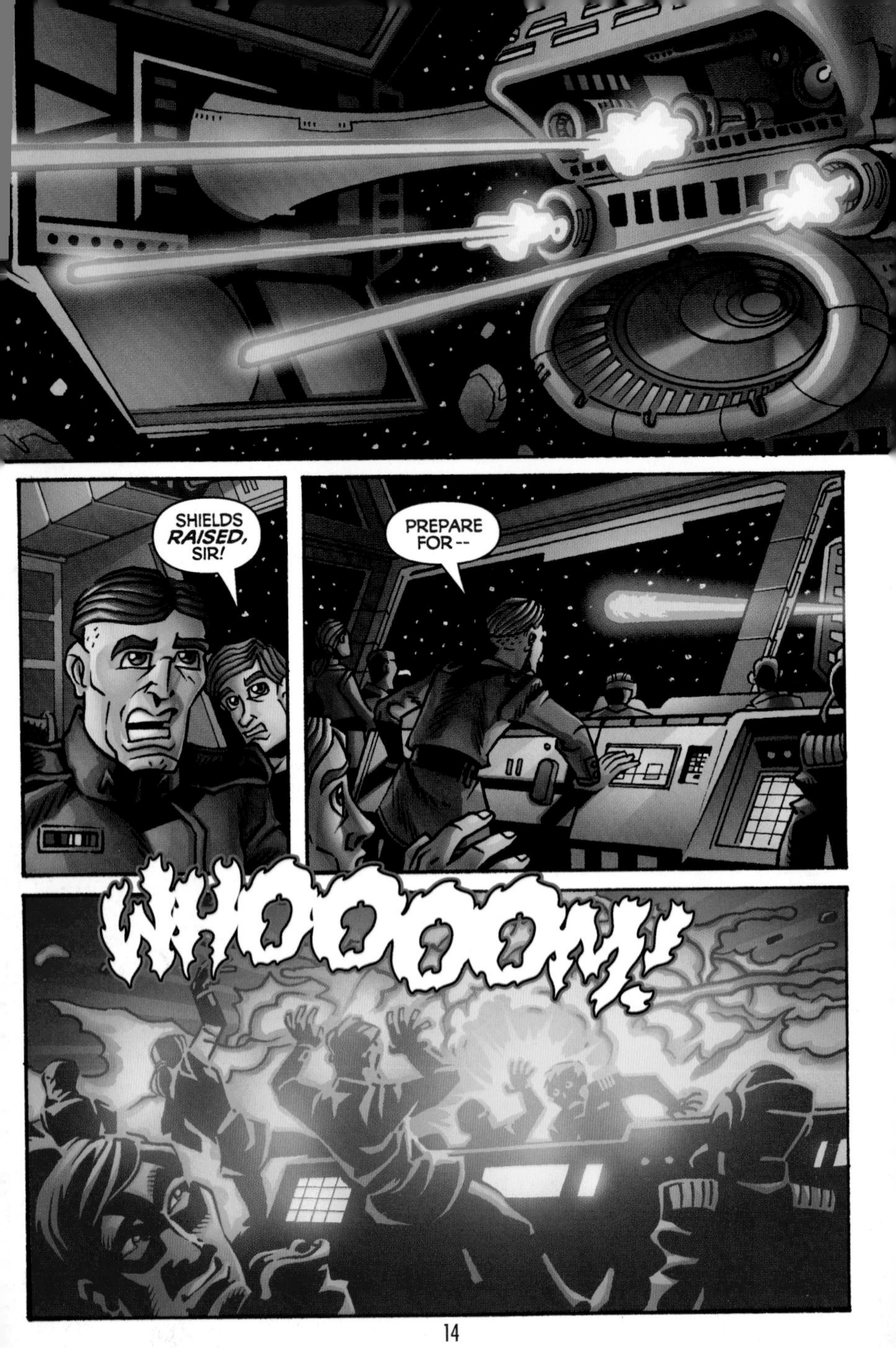
SHIELDS RAISED, SIR!
PREPARE FOR --
WHOOOOM!

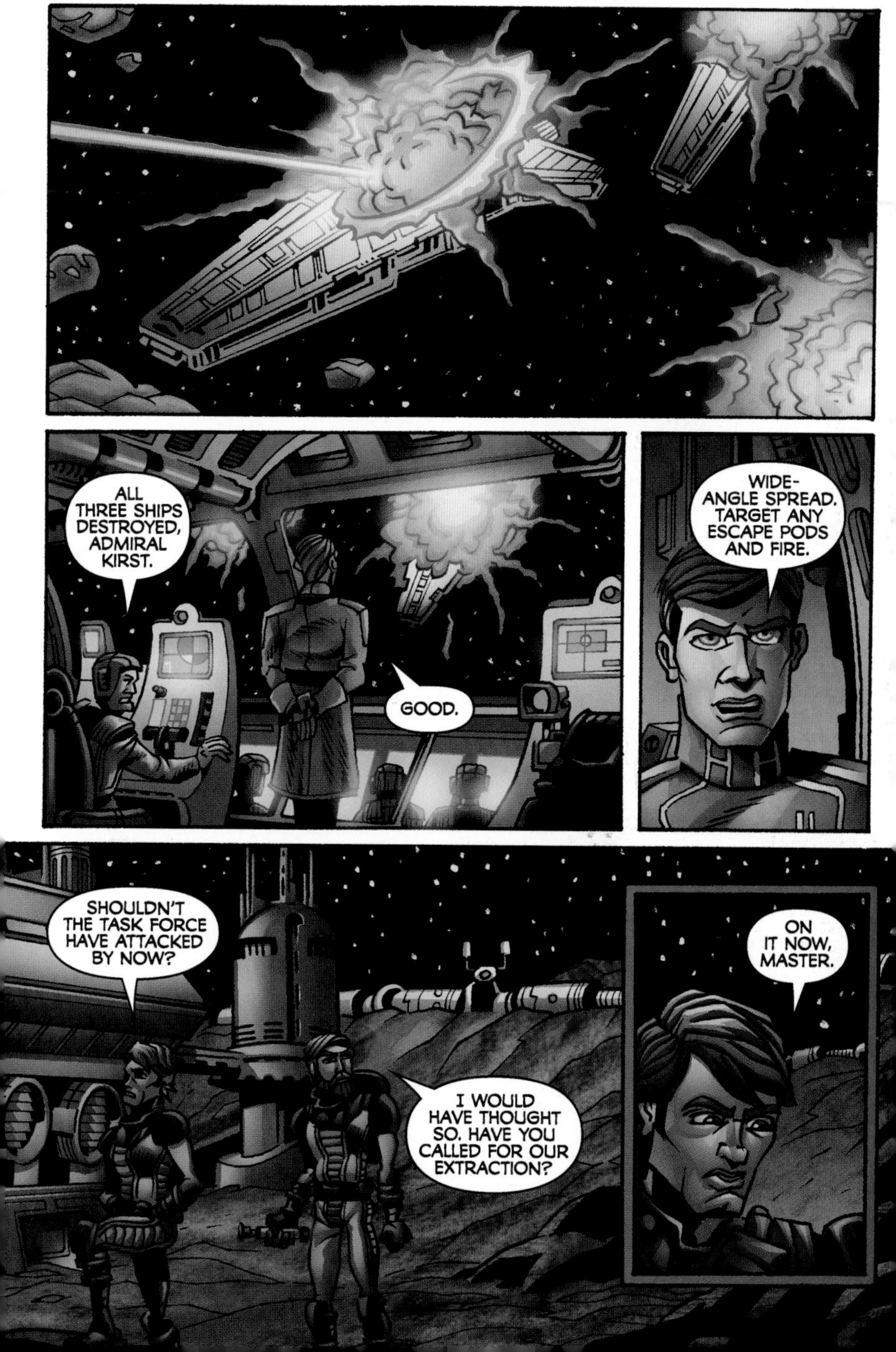
ALL THREE SHIPS DESTROYED, ADMIRAL KIRST.
GOOD.
WIDE-ANGLE SPREAD. TARGET ANY ESCAPE PODS AND FIRE.
SHOULDN'T THE TASK FORCE HAVE ATTACKED BY NOW?
I WOULD HAVE THOUGHT SO. HAVE YOU CALLED FOR OUR EXTRACTION?
ON IT NOW, MASTER.

AND HERE WE ARE.

GET ABOARD QUICKLY. I DON'T LIKE THIS!

YOU CALLED FOR A TAXI?

GET US OUT OF HERE, MASTER SOMTAY-- SOMETHING'S GONE WRONG!

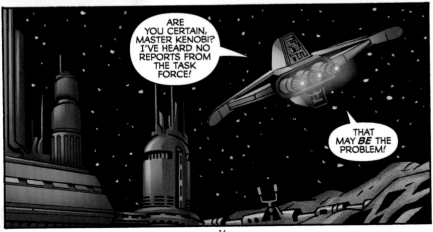

ARE YOU CERTAIN, MASTER KENOBI? I'VE HEARD NO REPORTS FROM THE TASK FORCE!

THAT MAY *BE* THE PROBLEM!

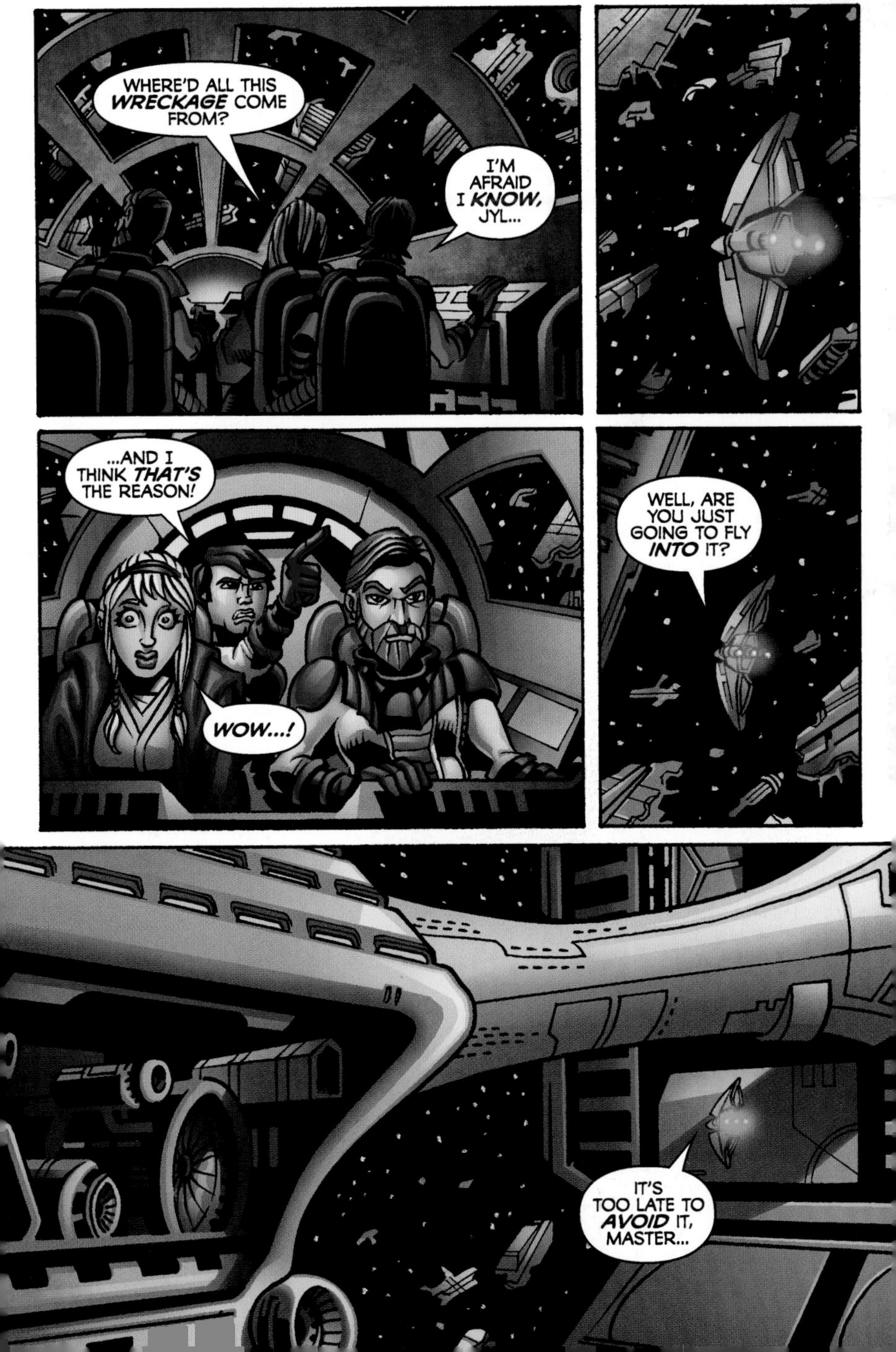

WHERE'D ALL THIS *WRECKAGE* COME FROM?
I'M AFRAID I *KNOW,* JYL...
...AND I THINK *THAT'S* THE REASON!
WOW...!
WELL, ARE YOU JUST GOING TO FLY *INTO* IT?
IT'S TOO LATE TO *AVOID* IT, MASTER...

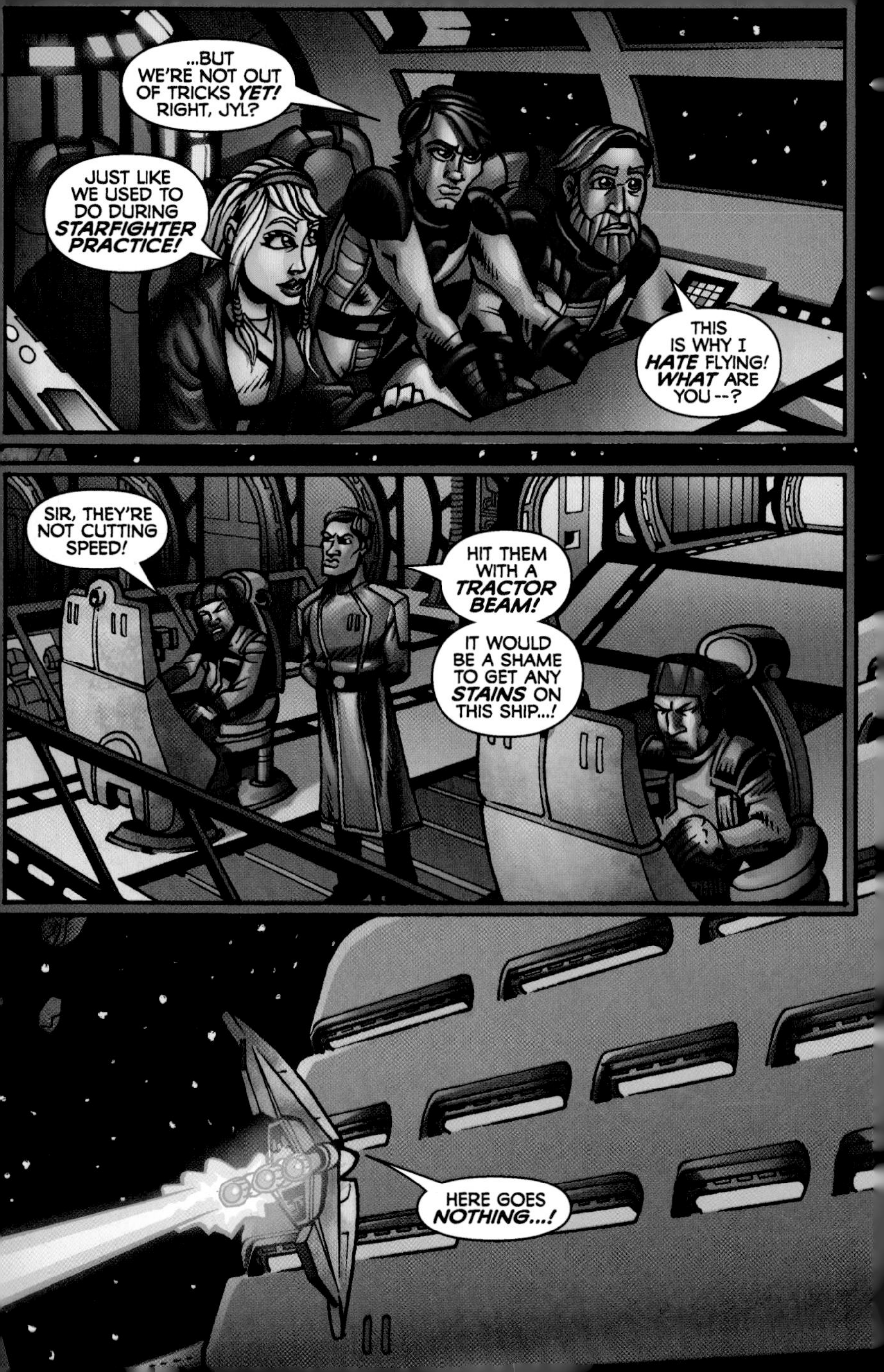
...BUT WE'RE NOT OUT OF TRICKS YET! RIGHT, JYL?
JUST LIKE WE USED TO DO DURING STARFIGHTER PRACTICE!
THIS IS WHY I HATE FLYING! WHAT ARE YOU--?
SIR, THEY'RE NOT CUTTING SPEED!
HIT THEM WITH A TRACTOR BEAM!
IT WOULD BE A SHAME TO GET ANY STAINS ON THIS SHIP...!
HERE GOES NOTHING...!

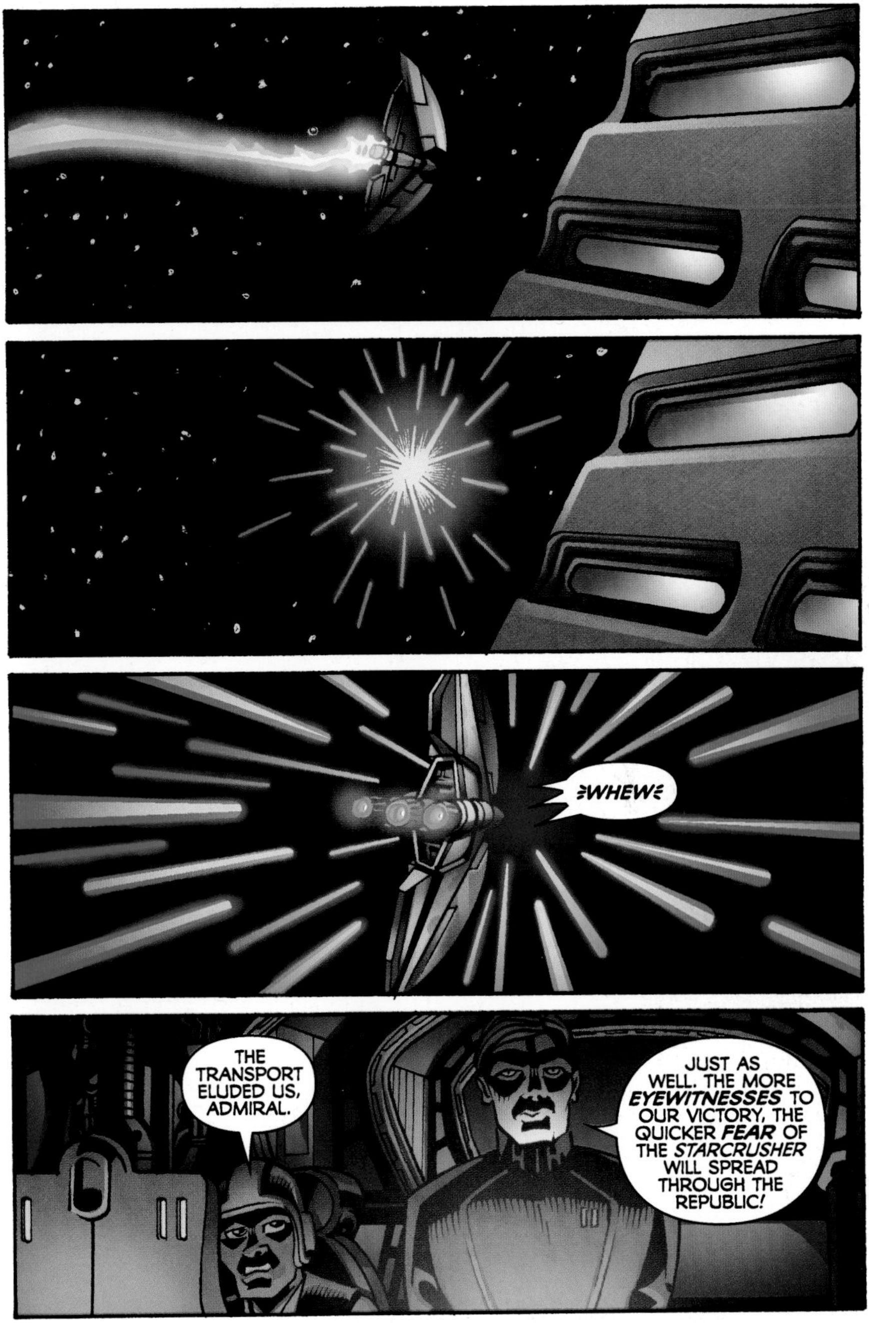
WHEW
THE TRANSPORT ELUDED US, ADMIRAL.
JUST AS WELL. THE MORE *EYEWITNESSES* TO OUR VICTORY, THE QUICKER *FEAR* OF THE *STARCRUSHER* WILL SPREAD THROUGH THE REPUBLIC!

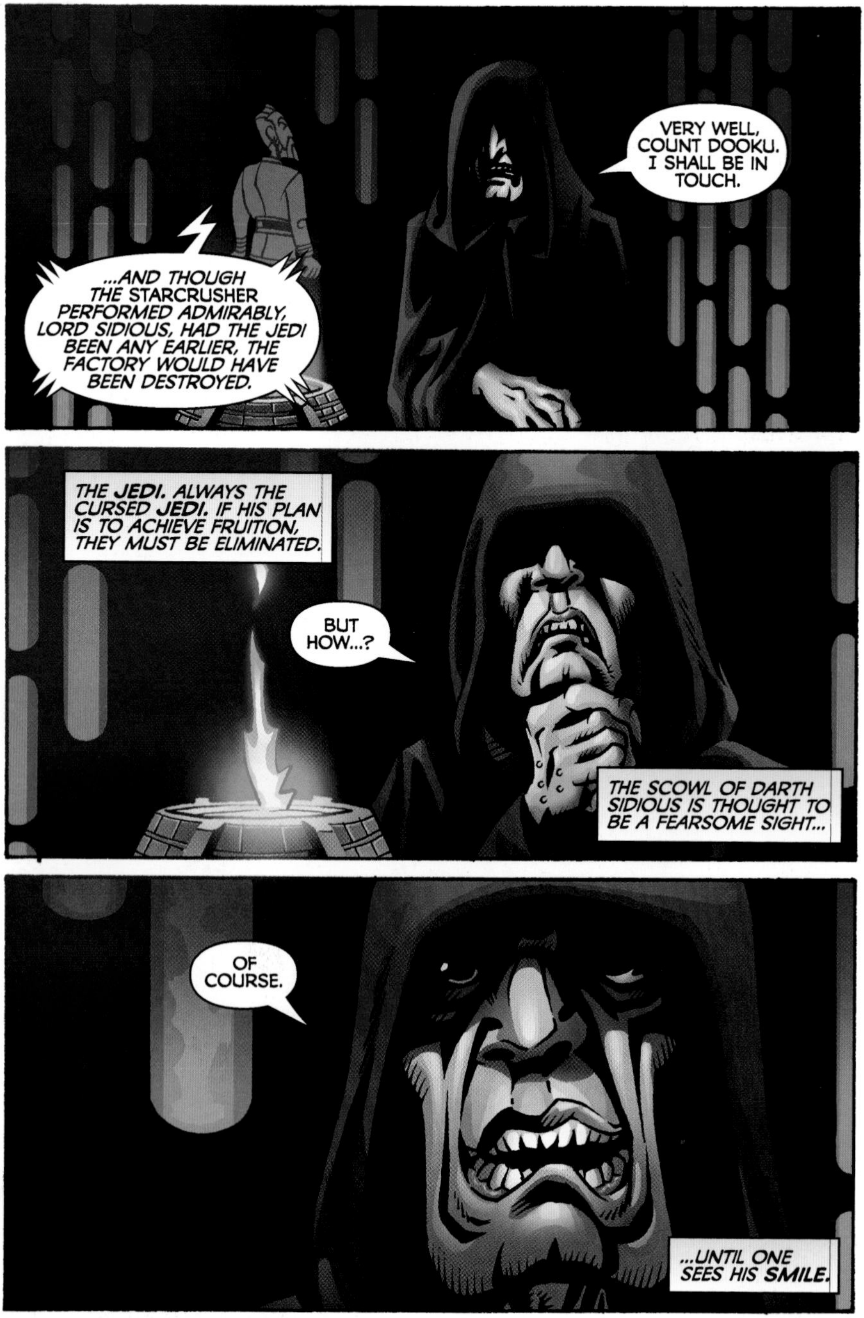
...AND THOUGH THE STARCRUSHER PERFORMED ADMIRABLY, LORD SIDIOUS, HAD THE JEDI BEEN ANY EARLIER, THE FACTORY WOULD HAVE BEEN DESTROYED.
VERY WELL, COUNT DOOKU. I SHALL BE IN TOUCH.
THE JEDI. ALWAYS THE CURSED JEDI. IF HIS PLAN IS TO ACHIEVE FRUITION, THEY MUST BE ELIMINATED.
BUT HOW...?
THE SCOWL OF DARTH SIDIOUS IS THOUGHT TO BE A FEARSOME SIGHT...
OF COURSE.
...UNTIL ONE SEES HIS SMILE.

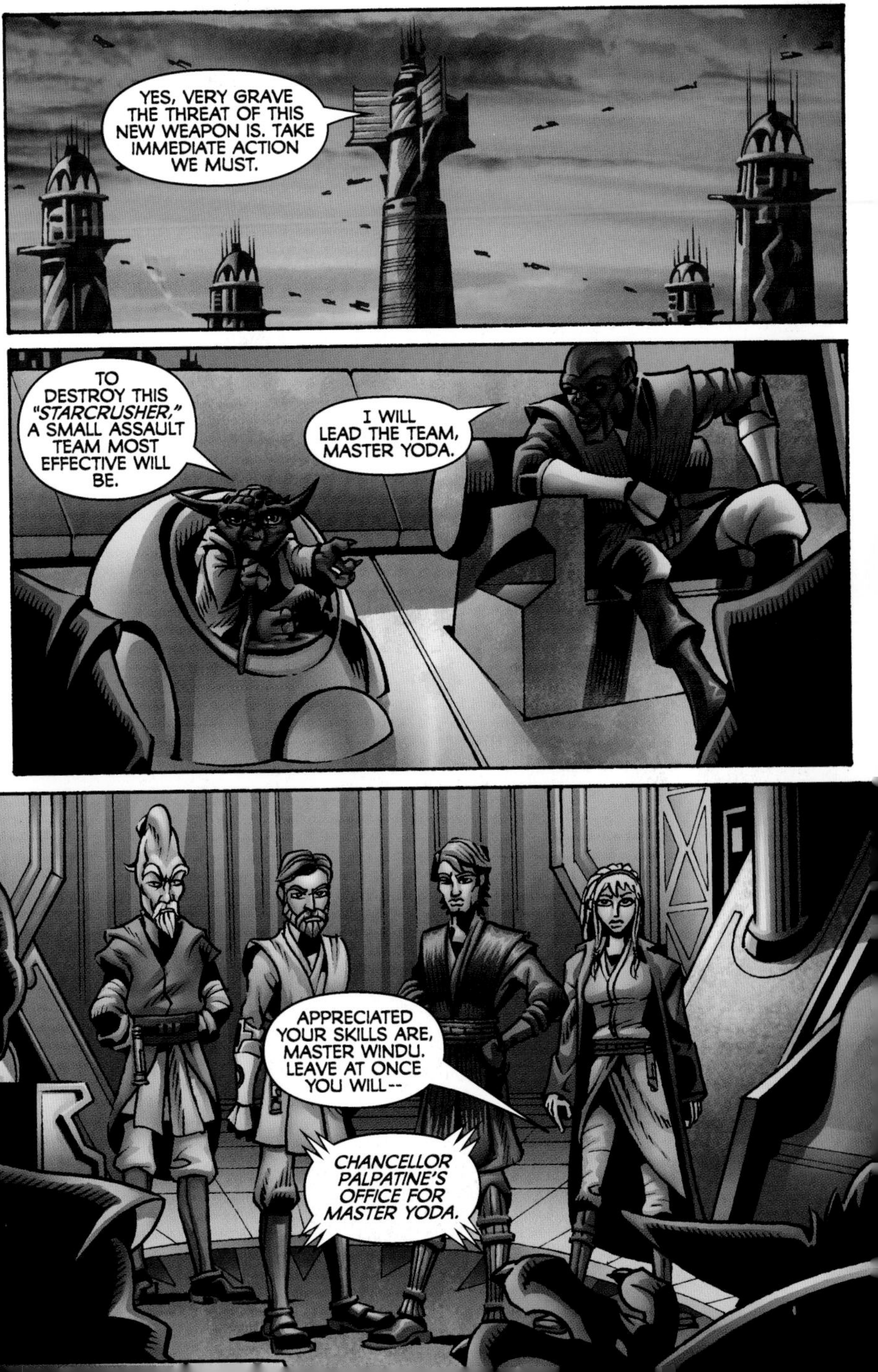
YES, VERY GRAVE THE THREAT OF THIS NEW WEAPON IS. TAKE IMMEDIATE ACTION WE MUST.
TO DESTROY THIS "STARCRUSHER," A SMALL ASSAULT TEAM MOST EFFECTIVE WILL BE.
I WILL LEAD THE TEAM, MASTER YODA.
APPRECIATED YOUR SKILLS ARE, MASTER WINDU. LEAVE AT ONCE YOU WILL--
CHANCELLOR PALPATINE'S OFFICE FOR MASTER YODA.

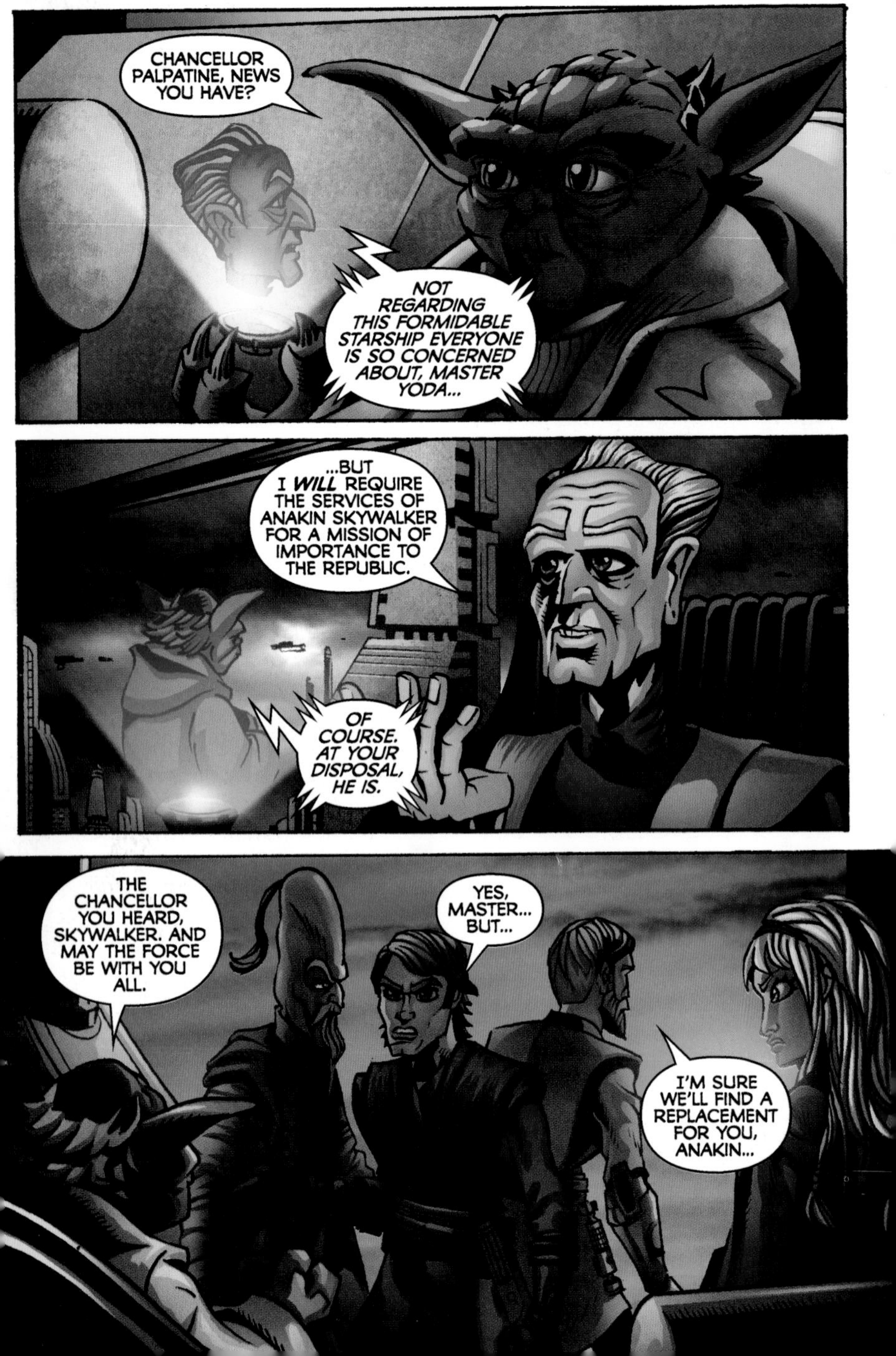
CHANCELLOR PALPATINE, NEWS YOU HAVE?
NOT REGARDING THIS FORMIDABLE STARSHIP EVERYONE IS SO CONCERNED ABOUT, MASTER YODA...
...BUT I *WILL* REQUIRE THE SERVICES OF ANAKIN SKYWALKER FOR A MISSION OF IMPORTANCE TO THE REPUBLIC.
OF COURSE. AT YOUR DISPOSAL, HE IS.
THE CHANCELLOR YOU HEARD, SKYWALKER. AND MAY THE FORCE BE WITH YOU ALL.
YES, MASTER... BUT...
I'M SURE WE'LL FIND A REPLACEMENT FOR YOU, ANAKIN...

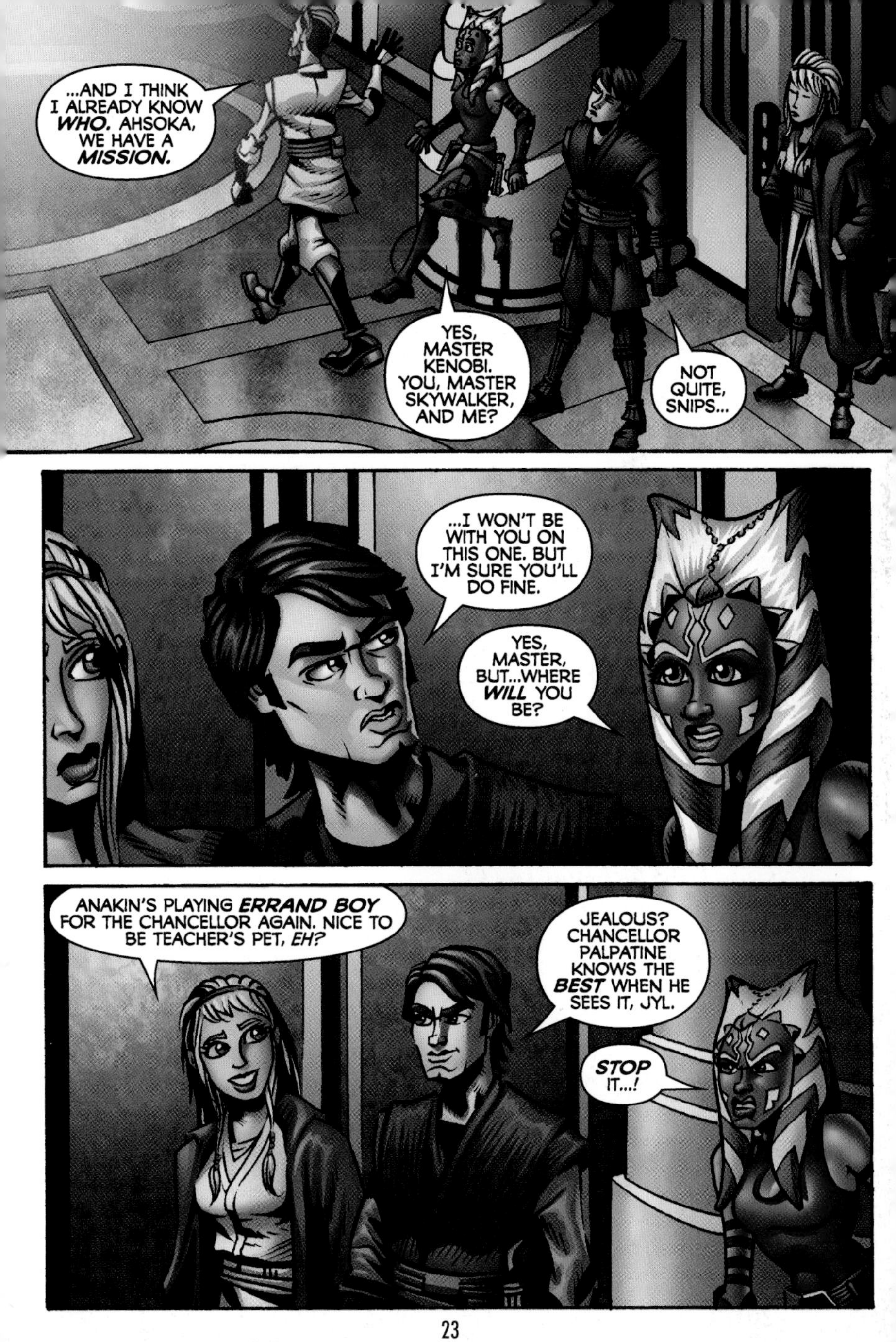
...AND I THINK I ALREADY KNOW WHO. AHSOKA, WE HAVE A MISSION.
YES, MASTER KENOBI. YOU, MASTER SKYWALKER, AND ME?
NOT QUITE, SNIPS...
...I WON'T BE WITH YOU ON THIS ONE. BUT I'M SURE YOU'LL DO FINE.
YES, MASTER, BUT...WHERE WILL YOU BE?
ANAKIN'S PLAYING ERRAND BOY FOR THE CHANCELLOR AGAIN. NICE TO BE TEACHER'S PET, EH?
JEALOUS? CHANCELLOR PALPATINE KNOWS THE BEST WHEN HE SEES IT, JYL.
STOP IT...!

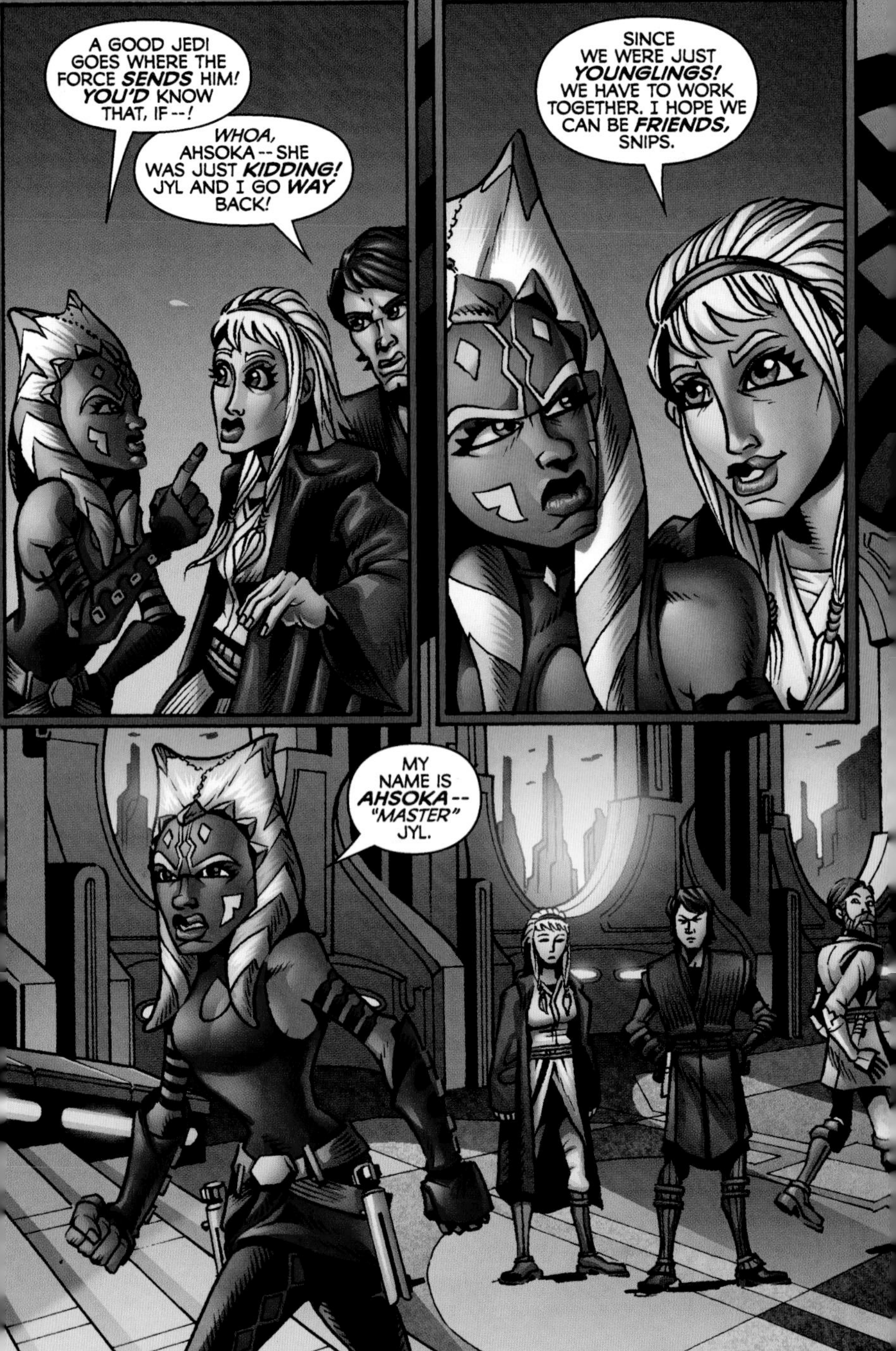
A GOOD JEDI GOES WHERE THE FORCE SENDS HIM! YOU'D KNOW THAT, IF--!
WHOA, AHSOKA--SHE WAS JUST KIDDING! JYL AND I GO WAY BACK!
SINCE WE WERE JUST YOUNGLINGS! WE HAVE TO WORK TOGETHER. I HOPE WE CAN BE FRIENDS, SNIPS.
MY NAME IS AHSOKA-- "MASTER" JYL.

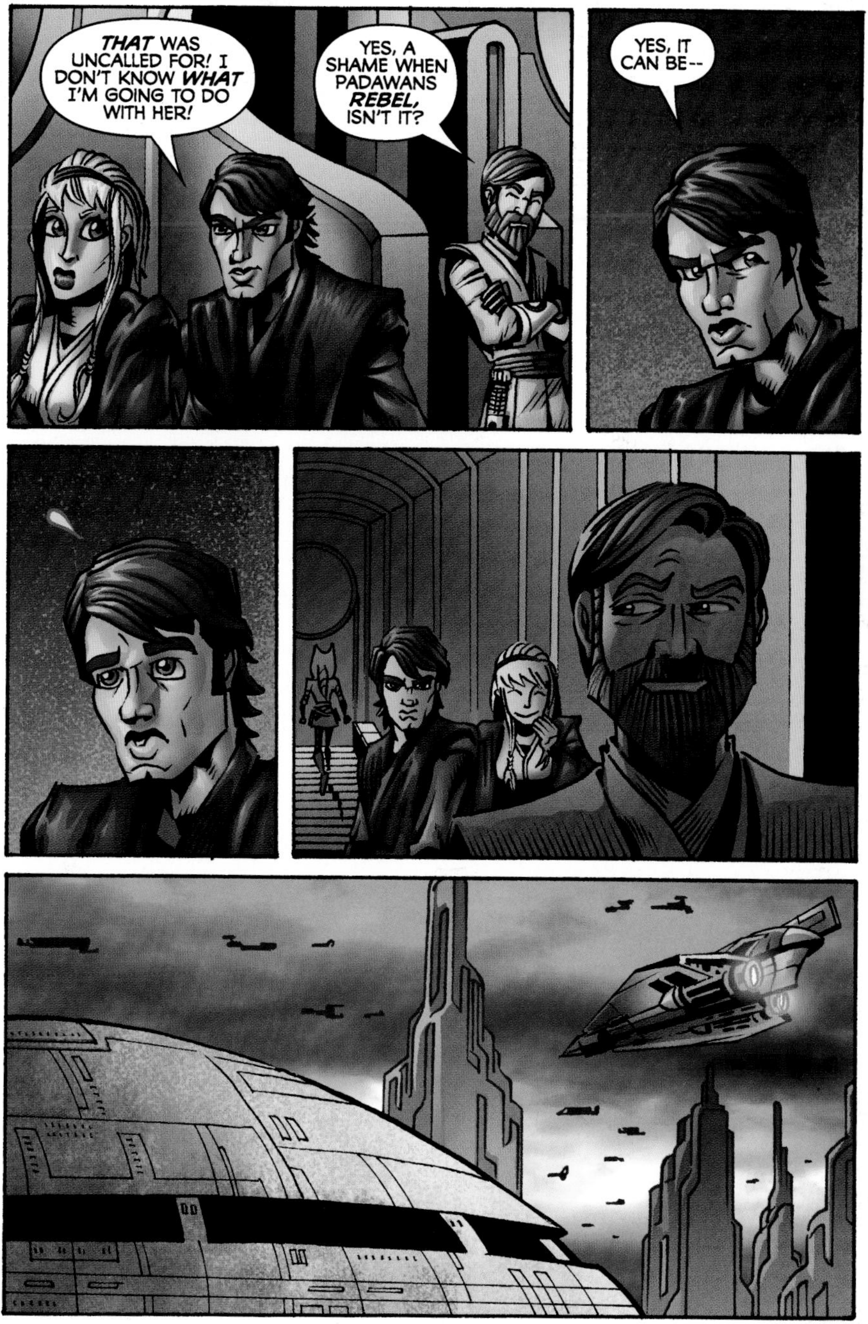
THAT WAS UNCALLED FOR! I DON'T KNOW WHAT I'M GOING TO DO WITH HER!
YES, A SHAME WHEN PADAWANS REBEL, ISN'T IT?
YES, IT CAN BE--

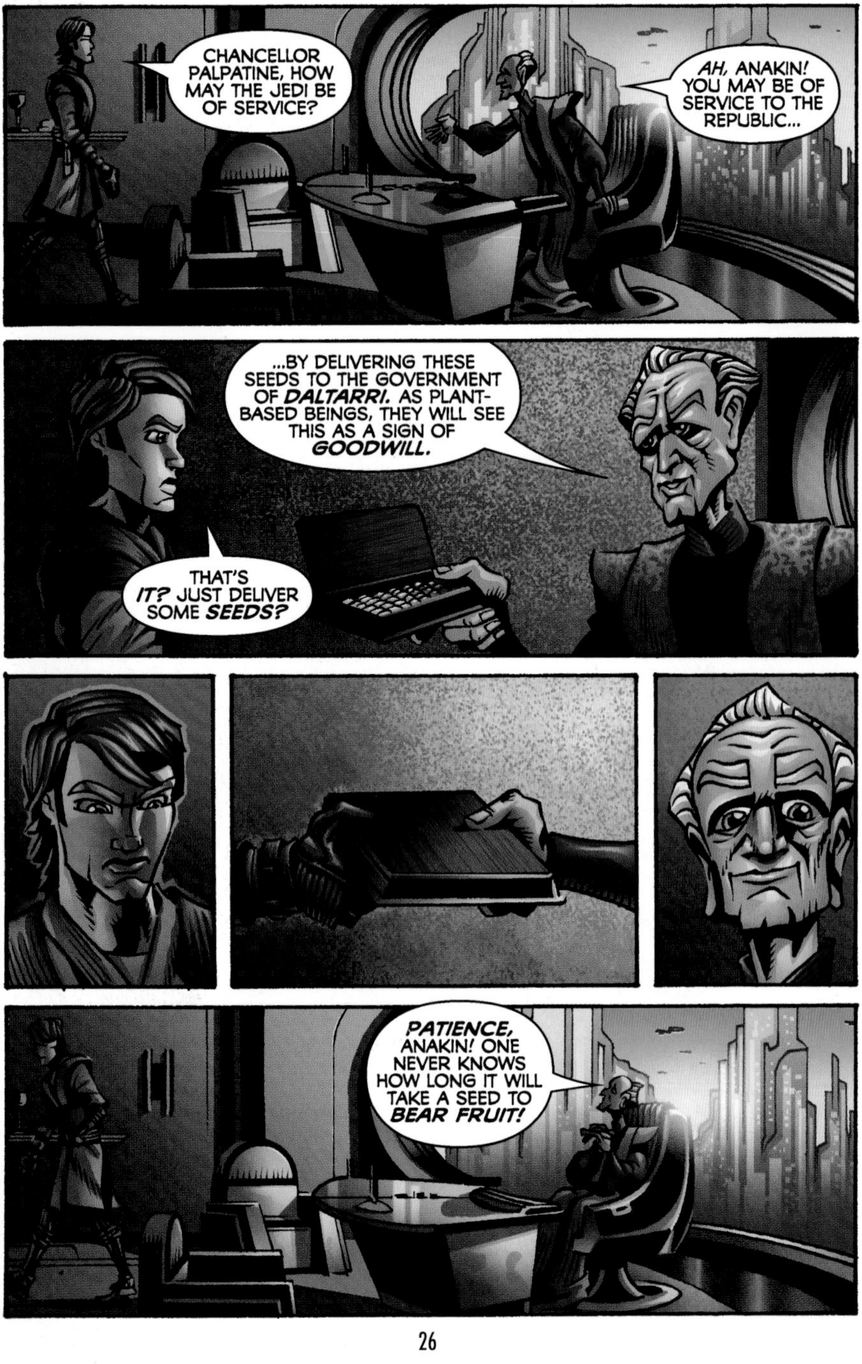
CHANCELLOR PALPATINE, HOW MAY THE JEDI BE OF SERVICE?
AH, ANAKIN! YOU MAY BE OF SERVICE TO THE REPUBLIC...
...BY DELIVERING THESE SEEDS TO THE GOVERNMENT OF DALTARRI. AS PLANT-BASED BEINGS, THEY WILL SEE THIS AS A SIGN OF GOODWILL.
THAT'S IT? JUST DELIVER SOME SEEDS?
PATIENCE, ANAKIN! ONE NEVER KNOWS HOW LONG IT WILL TAKE A SEED TO BEAR FRUIT!

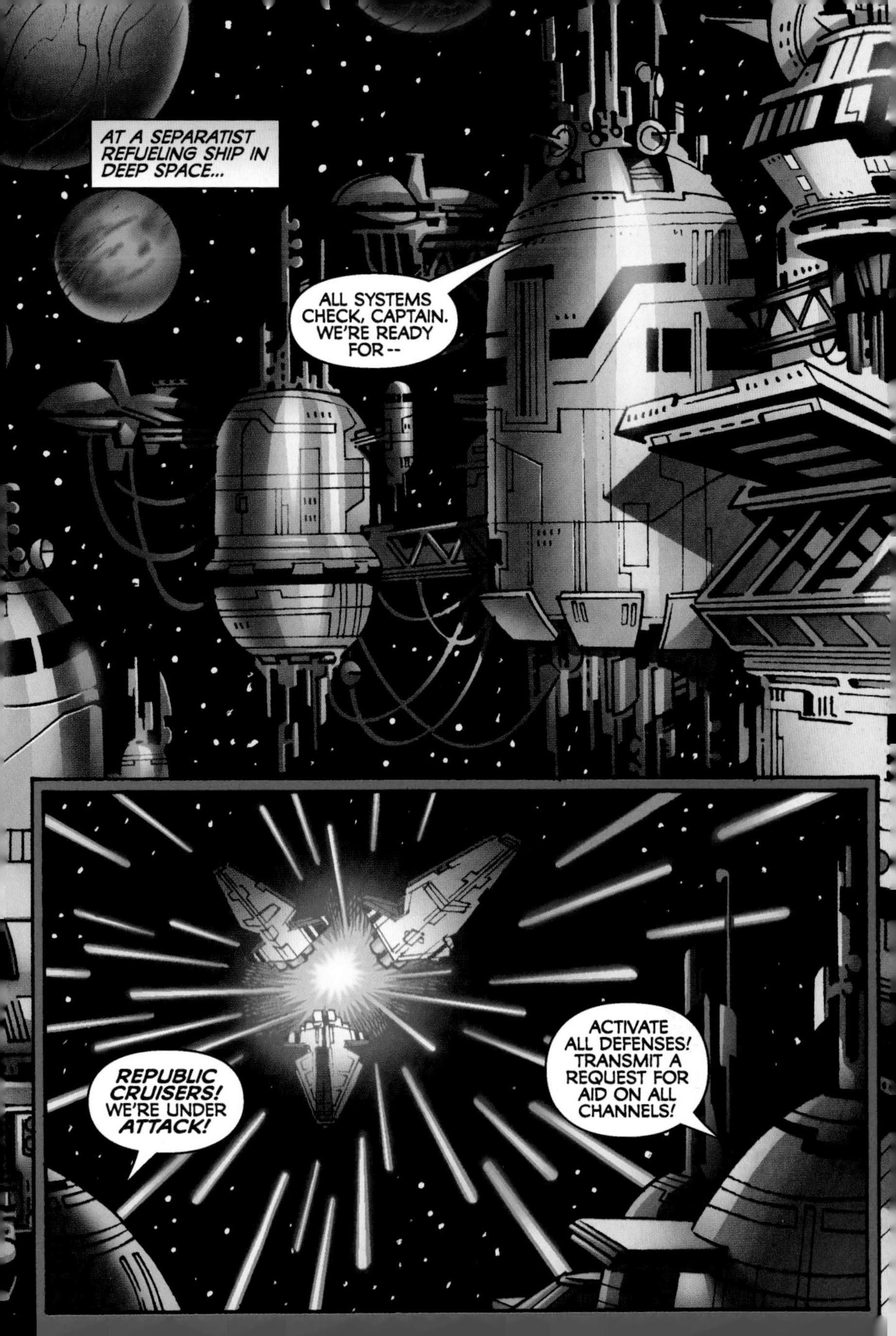
AT A SEPARATIST REFUELING SHIP IN DEEP SPACE...
ALL SYSTEMS CHECK, CAPTAIN. WE'RE READY FOR --
REPUBLIC CRUISERS! WE'RE UNDER ATTACK!
ACTIVATE ALL DEFENSES! TRANSMIT A REQUEST FOR AID ON ALL CHANNELS!

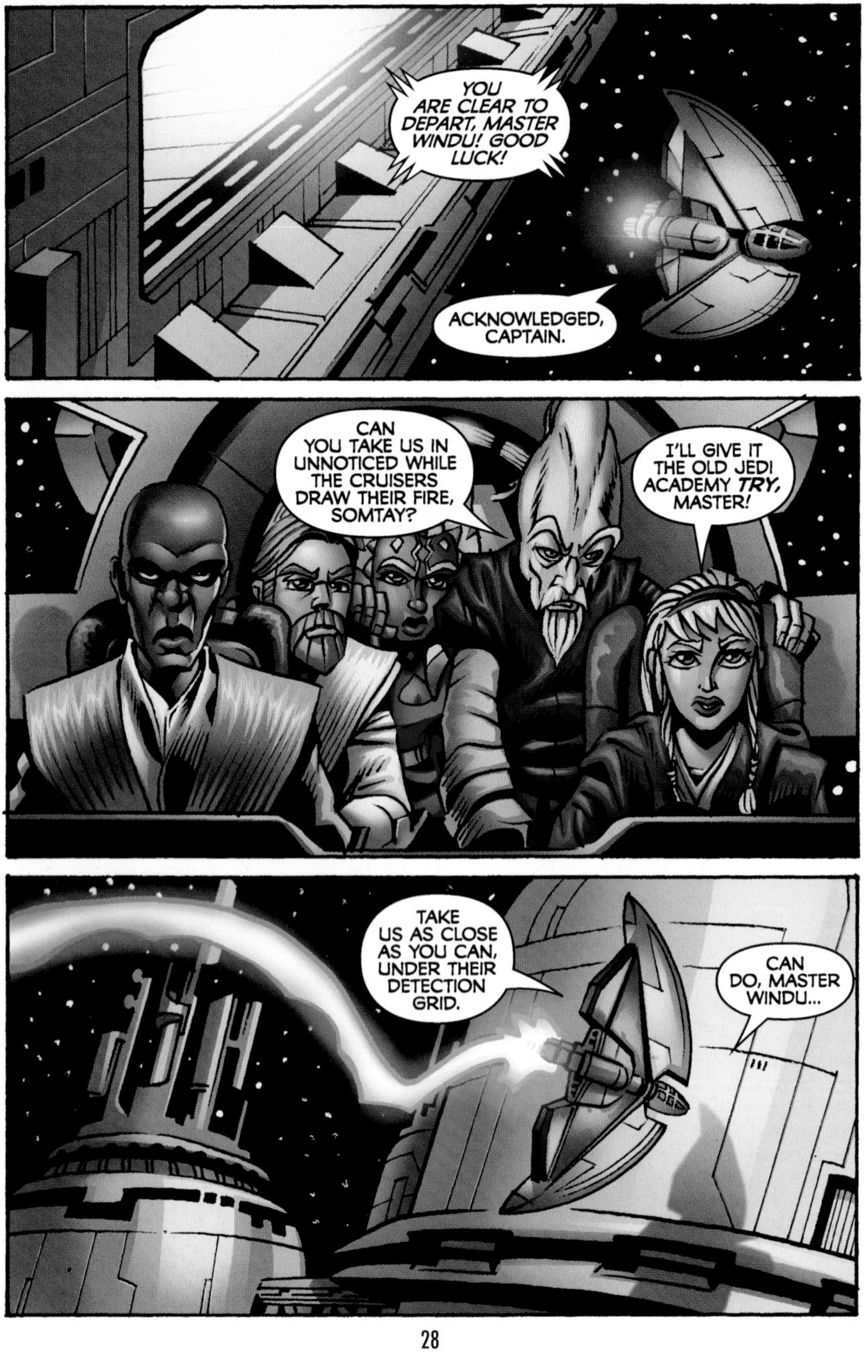
YOU ARE CLEAR TO DEPART, MASTER WINDU! GOOD LUCK!
ACKNOWLEDGED, CAPTAIN.
CAN YOU TAKE US IN UNNOTICED WHILE THE CRUISERS DRAW THEIR FIRE, SOMTAY?
I'LL GIVE IT THE OLD JEDI ACADEMY *TRY,* MASTER!
TAKE US AS CLOSE AS YOU CAN, UNDER THEIR DETECTION GRID.
CAN DO, MASTER WINDU...

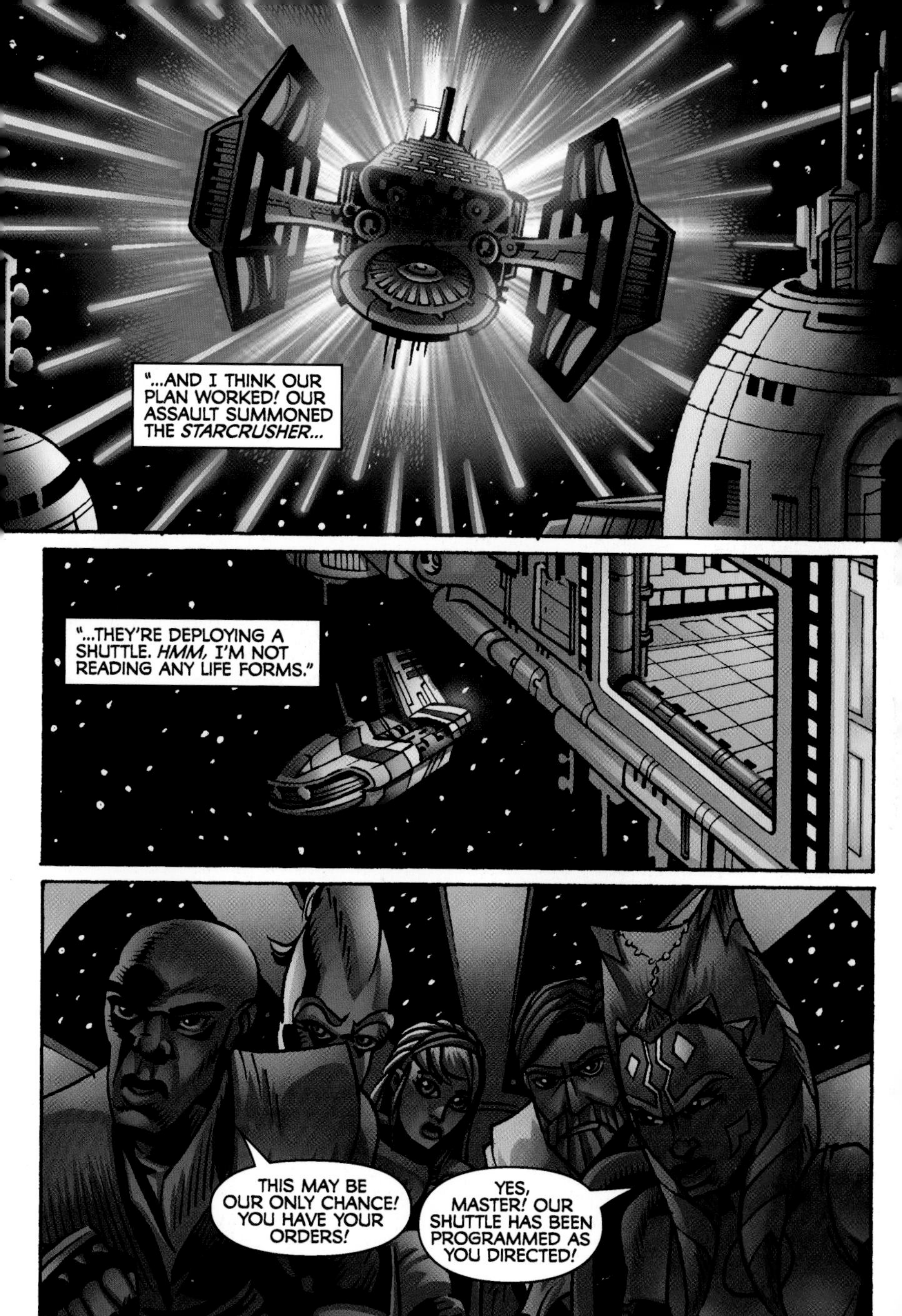
"...AND I THINK OUR PLAN WORKED! OUR ASSAULT SUMMONED THE *STARCRUSHER*...
"...THEY'RE DEPLOYING A SHUTTLE. *HMM,* I'M NOT READING ANY LIFE FORMS."
THIS MAY BE OUR ONLY CHANCE! YOU HAVE YOUR ORDERS!
YES, MASTER! OUR SHUTTLE HAS BEEN PROGRAMMED AS YOU DIRECTED!

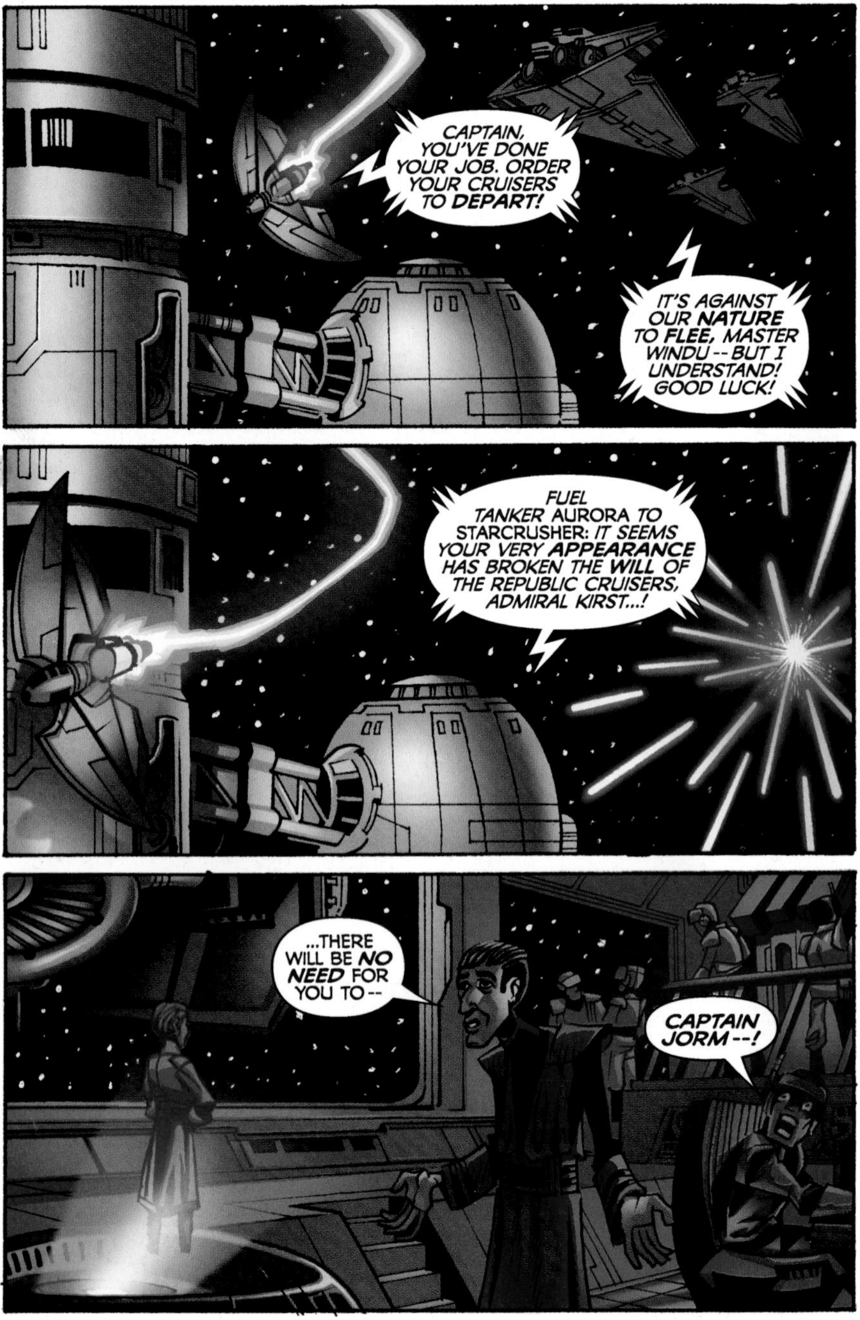
CAPTAIN, YOU'VE DONE YOUR JOB. ORDER YOUR CRUISERS TO DEPART!
IT'S AGAINST OUR NATURE TO FLEE, MASTER WINDU -- BUT I UNDERSTAND! GOOD LUCK!
FUEL TANKER AURORA TO STARCRUSHER: IT SEEMS YOUR VERY APPEARANCE HAS BROKEN THE WILL OF THE REPUBLIC CRUISERS, ADMIRAL KIRST...!
...THERE WILL BE NO NEED FOR YOU TO --
CAPTAIN JORM --!

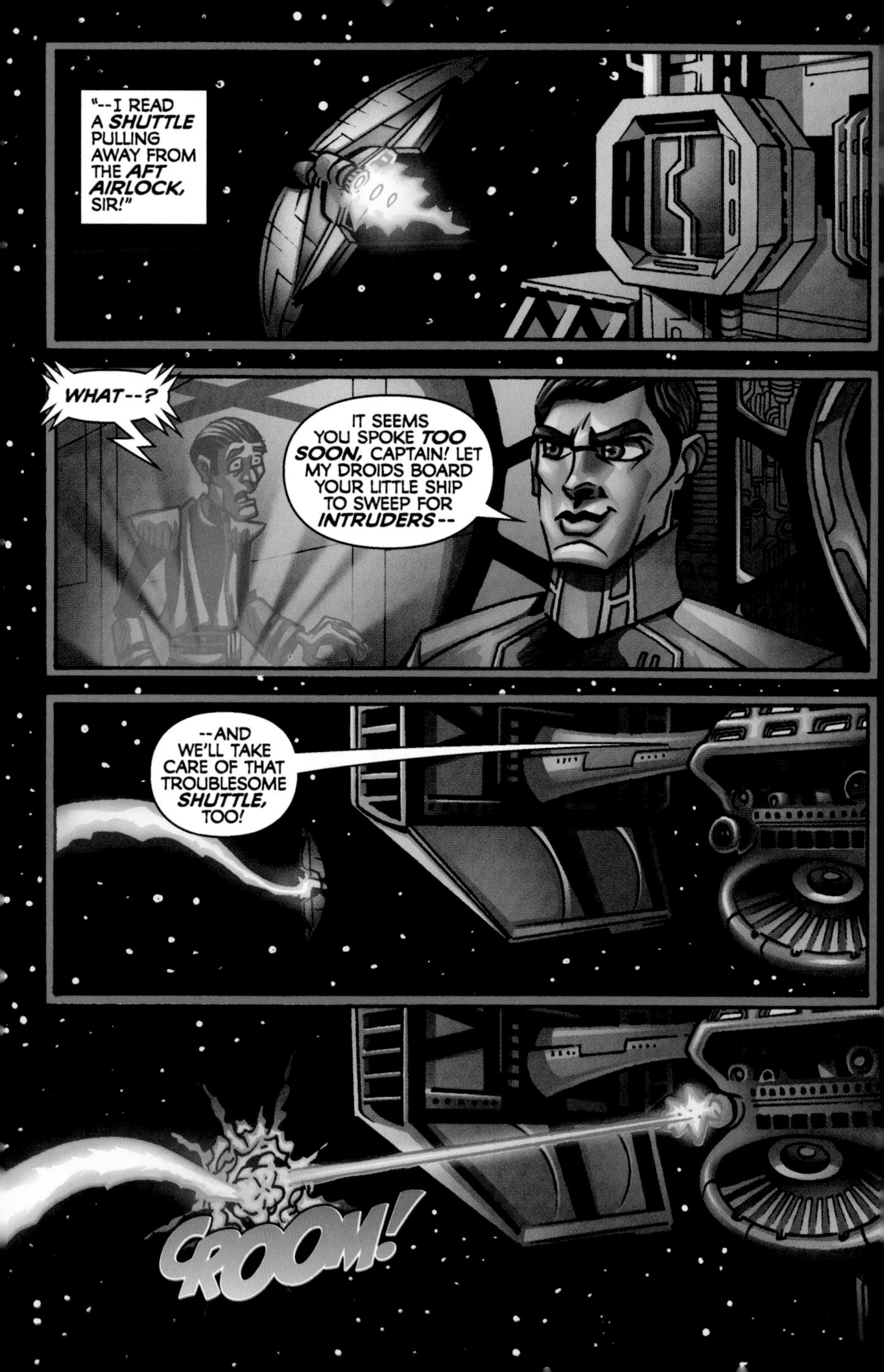
"--I READ A SHUTTLE PULLING AWAY FROM THE AFT AIRLOCK, SIR!"
WHAT--?
IT SEEMS YOU SPOKE TOO SOON, CAPTAIN! LET MY DROIDS BOARD YOUR LITTLE SHIP TO SWEEP FOR INTRUDERS--
--AND WE'LL TAKE CARE OF THAT TROUBLESOME SHUTTLE, TOO!
CROOM!

WELCOME TO OUR SHIP. WILL YOU NEED ANY ASSIS-TANCE--?
OOF! ALL RIGHT, THEN!
VMMMMMMMMMMMMM
CRSSSSH!
VMMMMM!
KRZZZZT!

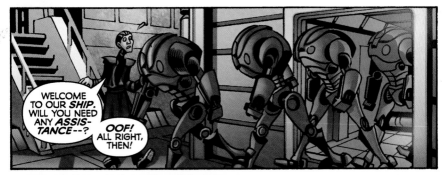

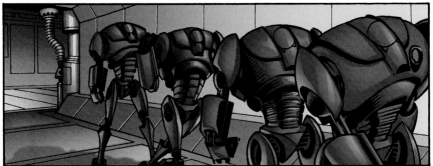

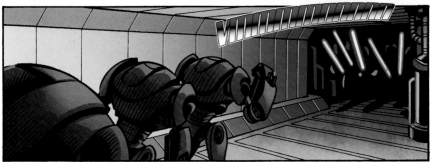

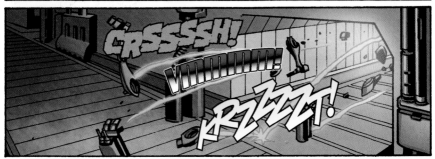

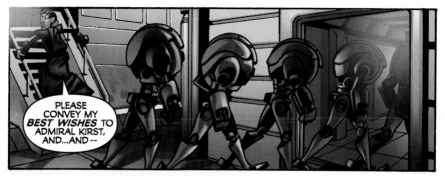

PLEASE CONVEY MY *BEST WISHES* TO ADMIRAL KIRST, AND...AND --

MY, *THEY* WERE CERTAINLY RUDE! PREPARE TO LEAVE THE SYSTEM!

THE DROIDS ARE RETURNING, ADMIRAL KIRST. THEIR DOWNLOAD READS NO REPORT WITH HOSTILES.

I *KNEW* IT! WHATEVER THE REPUBLIC WAS ATTEMPTING, IT *DIED* WITH THEIR SHUTTLE!

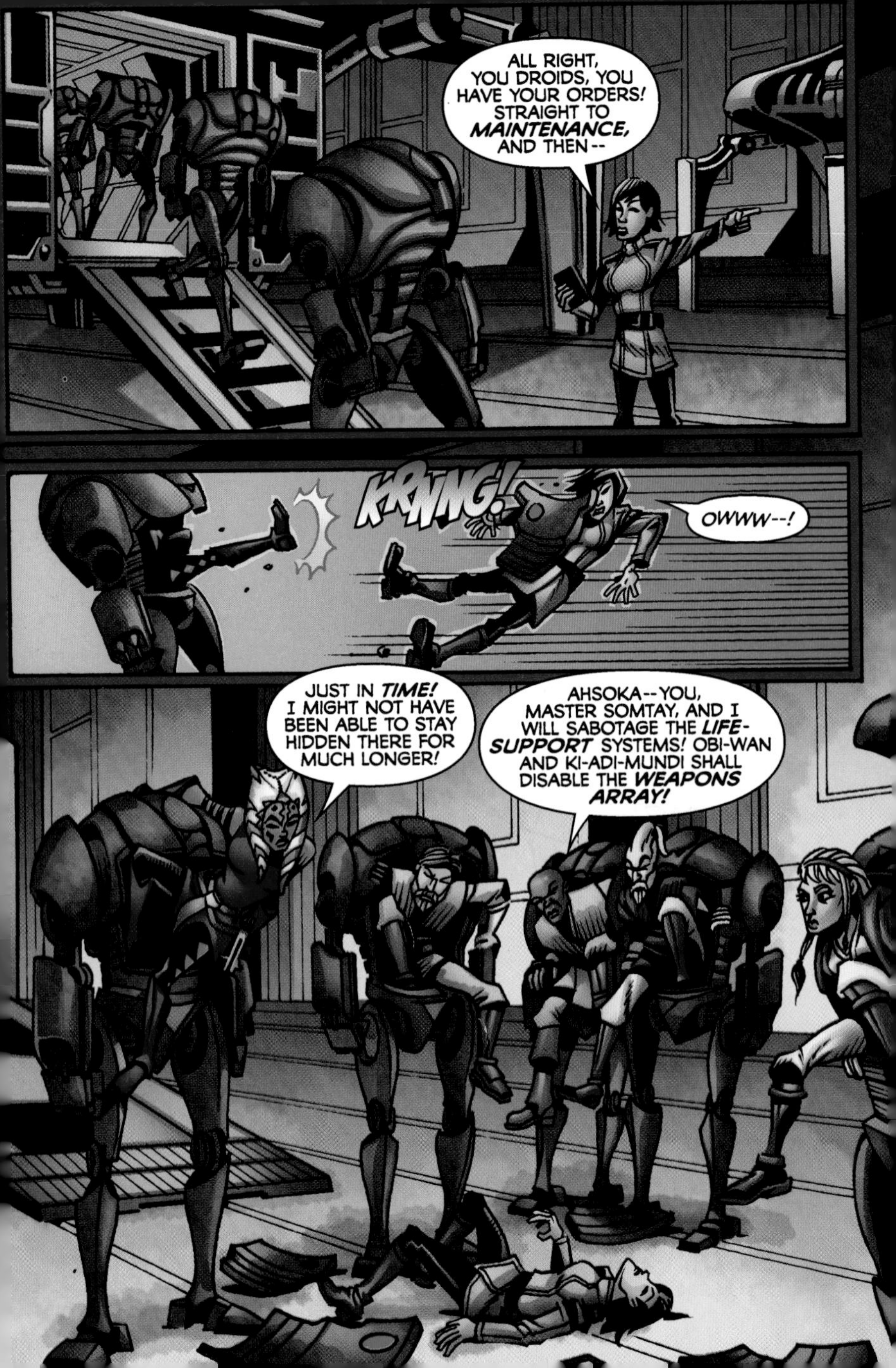
ALL RIGHT, YOU DROIDS, YOU HAVE YOUR ORDERS! STRAIGHT TO MAINTENANCE, AND THEN--
K-RNNG!
OWWW--!
JUST IN TIME! I MIGHT NOT HAVE BEEN ABLE TO STAY HIDDEN THERE FOR MUCH LONGER!
AHSOKA--YOU, MASTER SOMTAY, AND I WILL SABOTAGE THE LIFE-SUPPORT SYSTEMS! OBI-WAN AND KI-ADI-MUNDI SHALL DISABLE THE WEAPONS ARRAY!

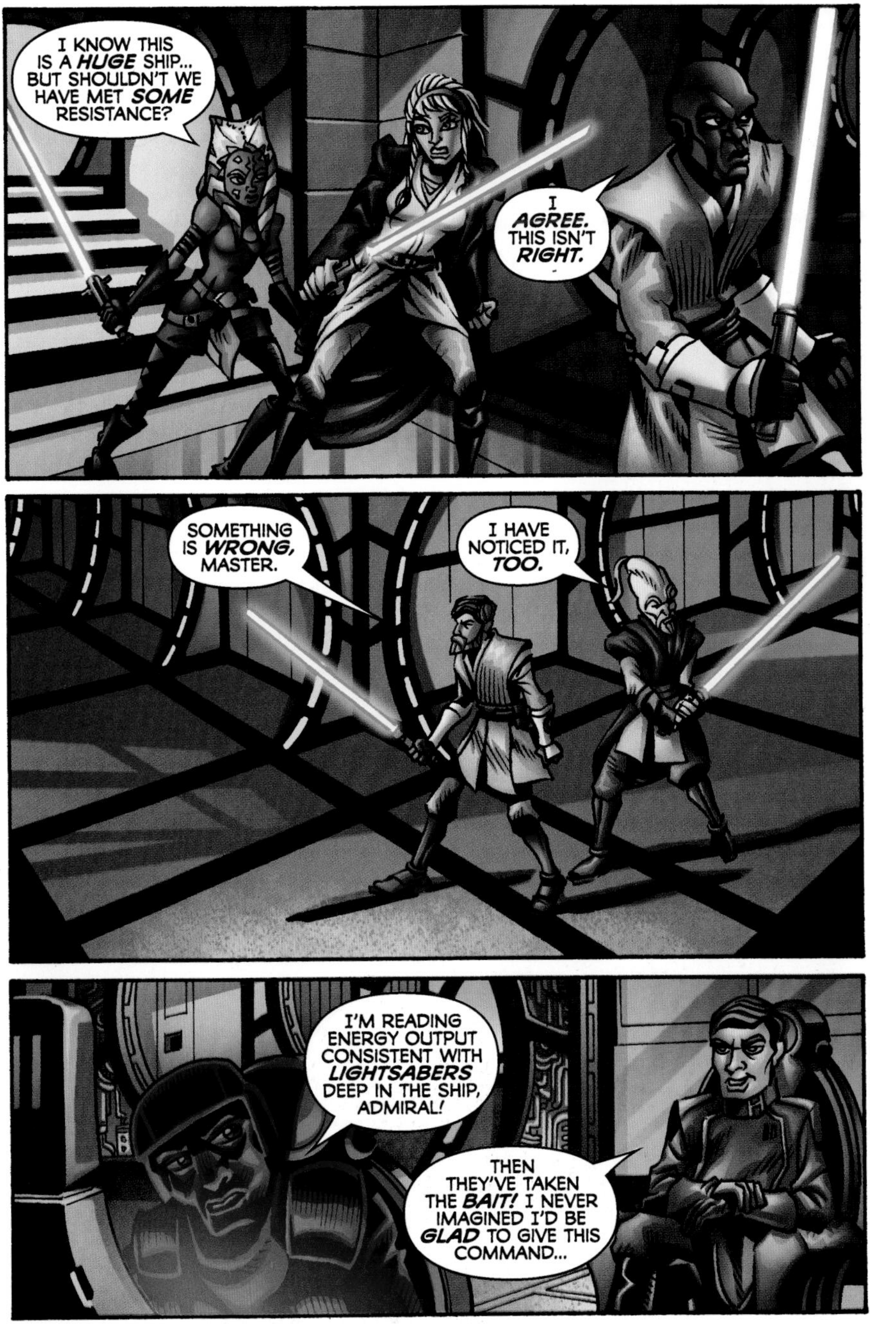
I KNOW THIS IS A *HUGE* SHIP... BUT SHOULDN'T WE HAVE MET *SOME* RESISTANCE?
I *AGREE.* THIS ISN'T *RIGHT.*
SOMETHING IS *WRONG,* MASTER.
I HAVE NOTICED IT, *TOO.*
I'M READING ENERGY OUTPUT CONSISTENT WITH *LIGHTSABERS* DEEP IN THE SHIP, ADMIRAL!
THEN THEY'VE TAKEN THE *BAIT!* I NEVER IMAGINED I'D BE *GLAD* TO GIVE THIS COMMAND...

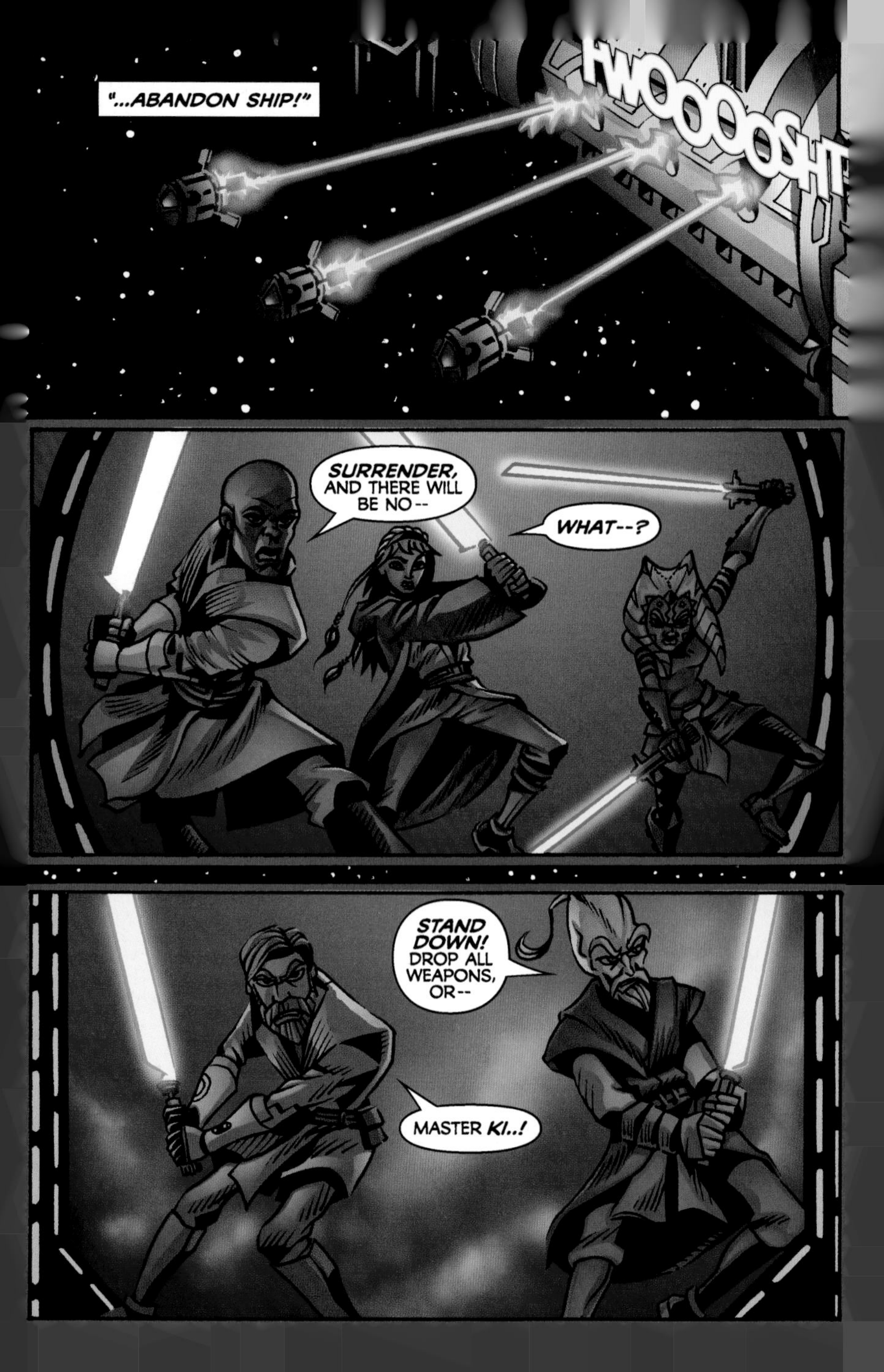
"...ABANDON SHIP!"
FWOOOOSH
SURRENDER, AND THERE WILL BE NO--
WHAT--?
STAND DOWN! DROP ALL WEAPONS, OR--
MASTER KI..!

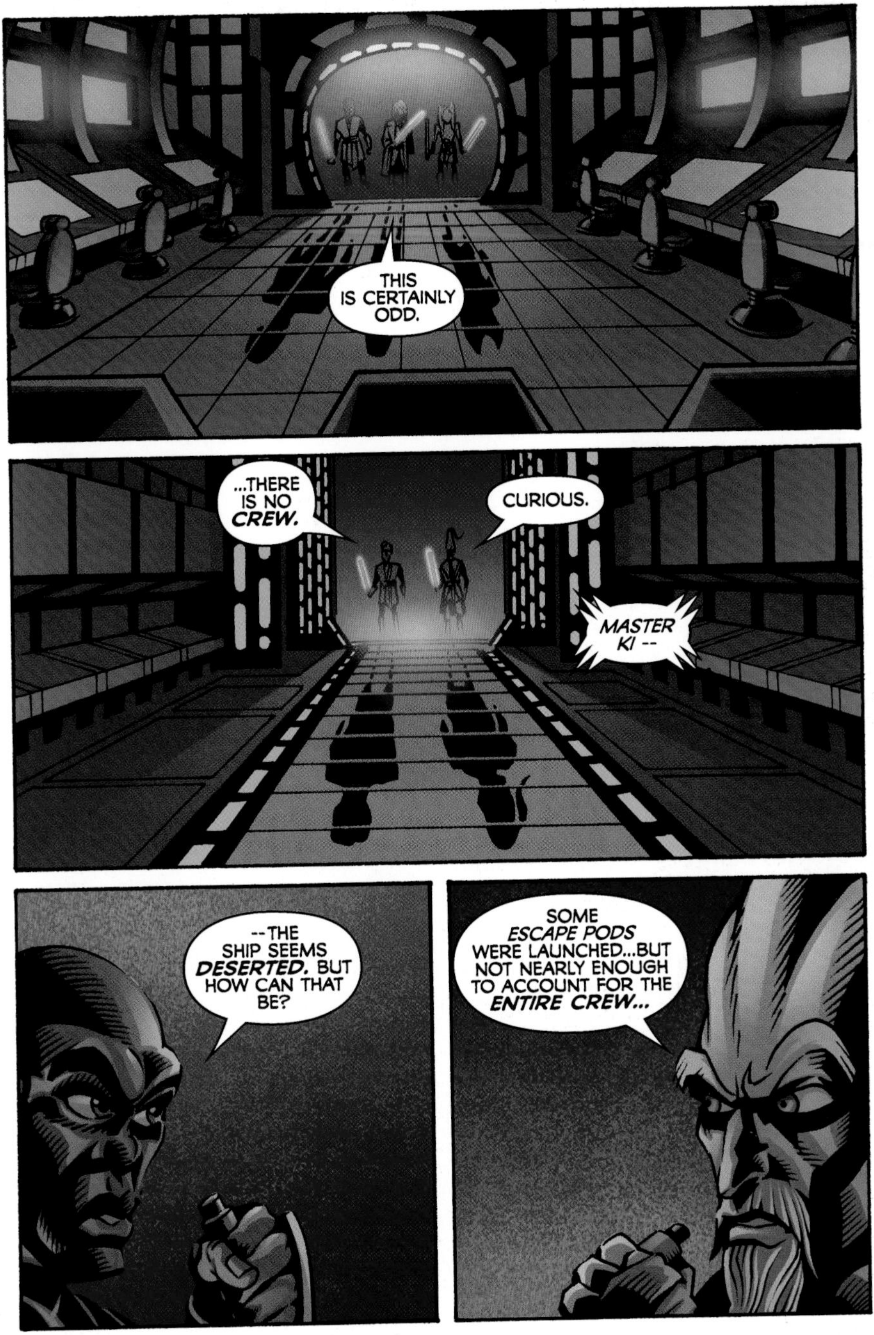
THIS IS CERTAINLY ODD.
...THERE IS NO CREW.
CURIOUS.
MASTER KI --
--THE SHIP SEEMS DESERTED. BUT HOW CAN THAT BE?
SOME ESCAPE PODS WERE LAUNCHED...BUT NOT NEARLY ENOUGH TO ACCOUNT FOR THE ENTIRE CREW...

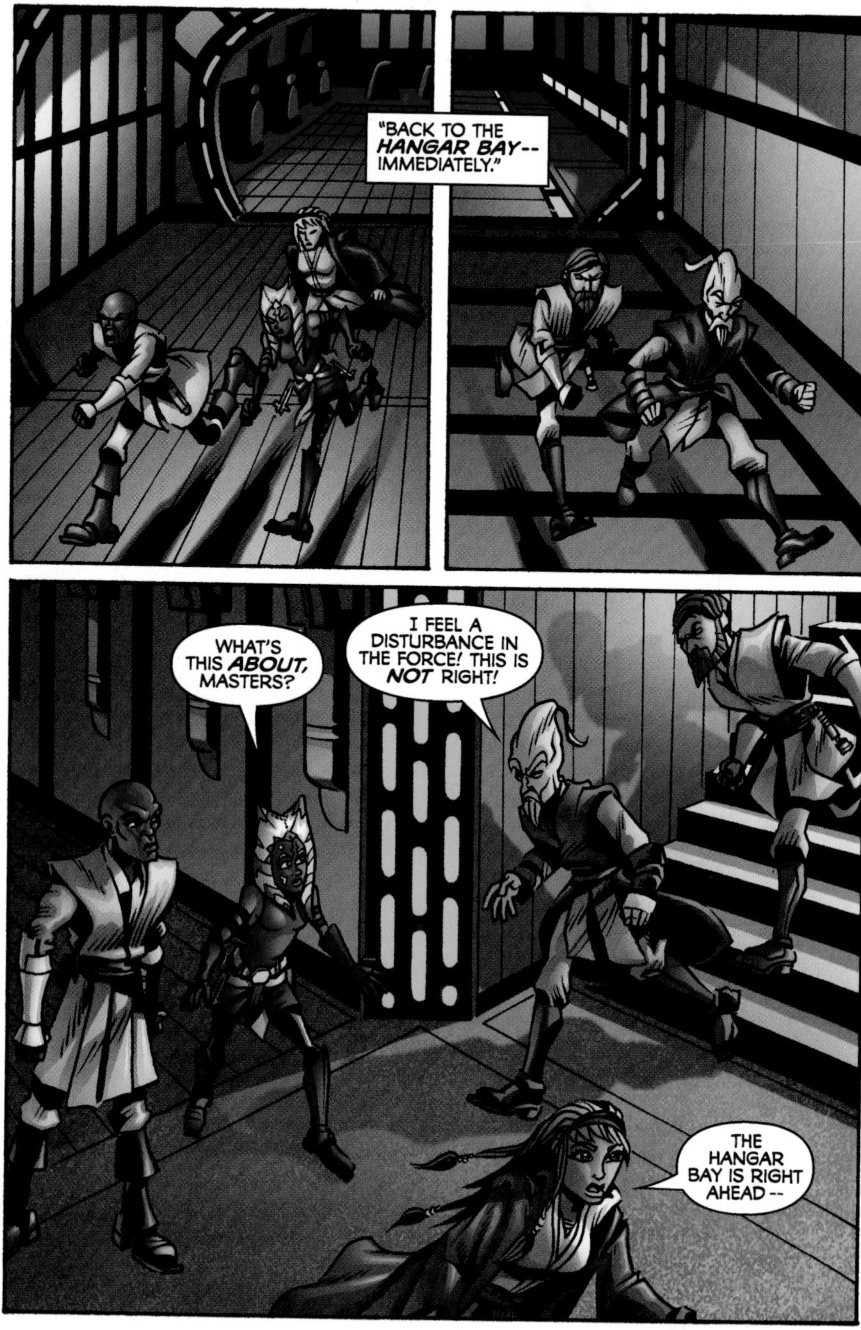
"BACK TO THE HANGAR BAY-- IMMEDIATELY."
WHAT'S THIS ABOUT, MASTERS?
I FEEL A DISTURBANCE IN THE FORCE! THIS IS NOT RIGHT!
THE HANGAR BAY IS RIGHT AHEAD --

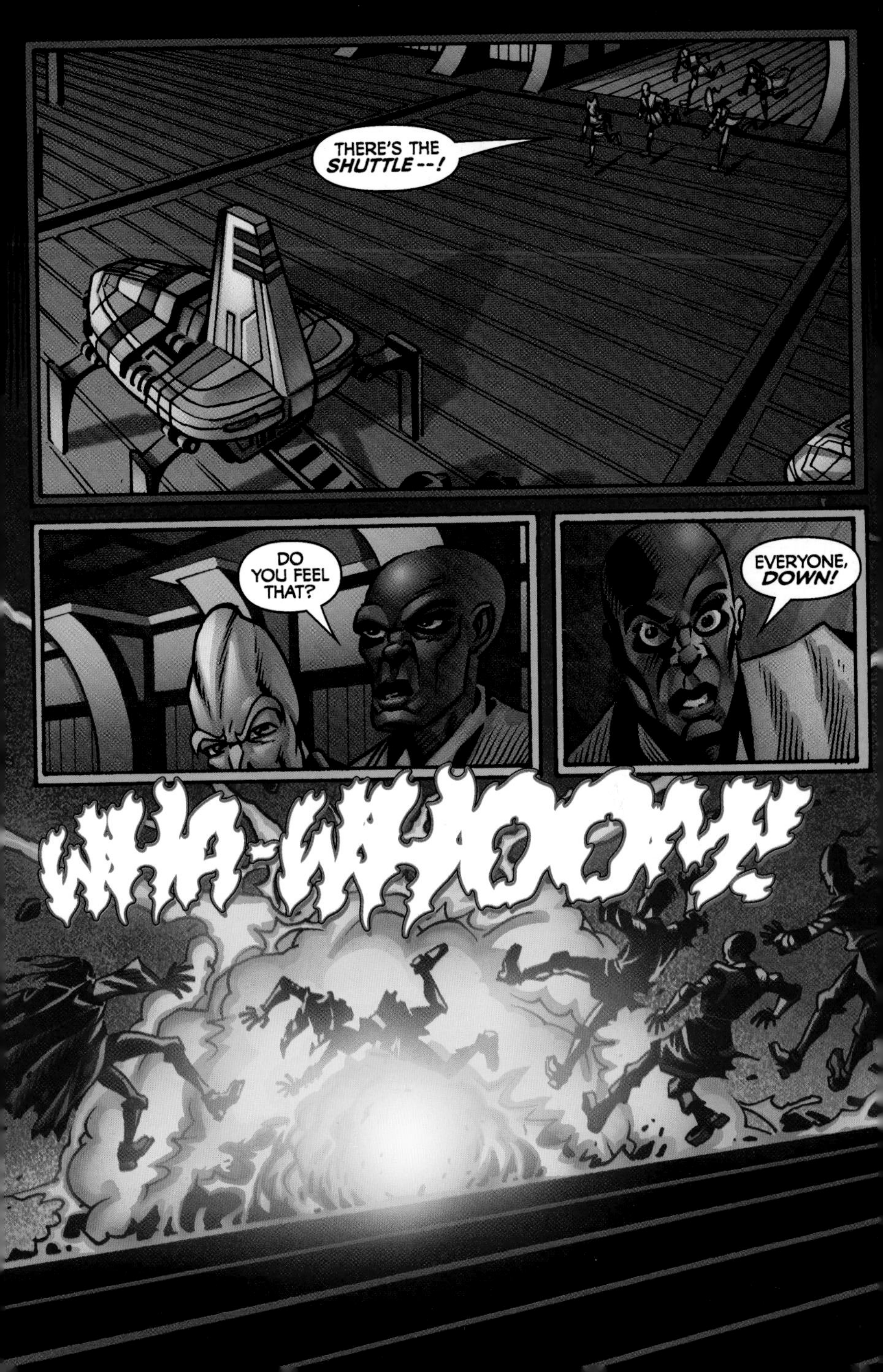
THERE'S THE SHUTTLE--!
DO YOU FEEL THAT?
EVERYONE, DOWN!
WHA-WHOOM!

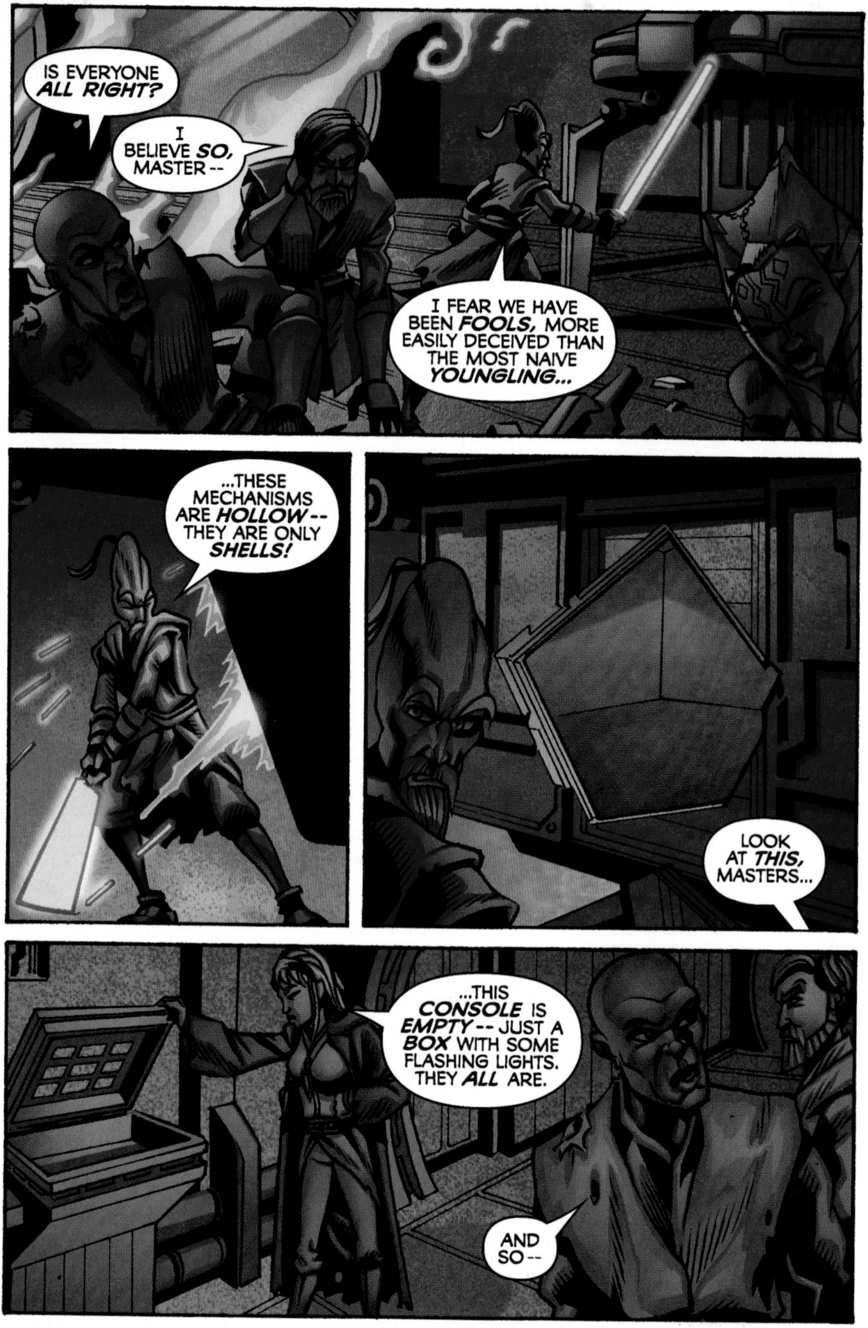

IS EVERYONE ALL RIGHT?
I BELIEVE SO, MASTER --
I FEAR WE HAVE BEEN FOOLS, MORE EASILY DECEIVED THAN THE MOST NAIVE YOUNGLING...
...THESE MECHANISMS ARE HOLLOW -- THEY ARE ONLY SHELLS!
LOOK AT THIS, MASTERS...
...THIS CONSOLE IS EMPTY -- JUST A BOX WITH SOME FLASHING LIGHTS. THEY ALL ARE.
AND SO --

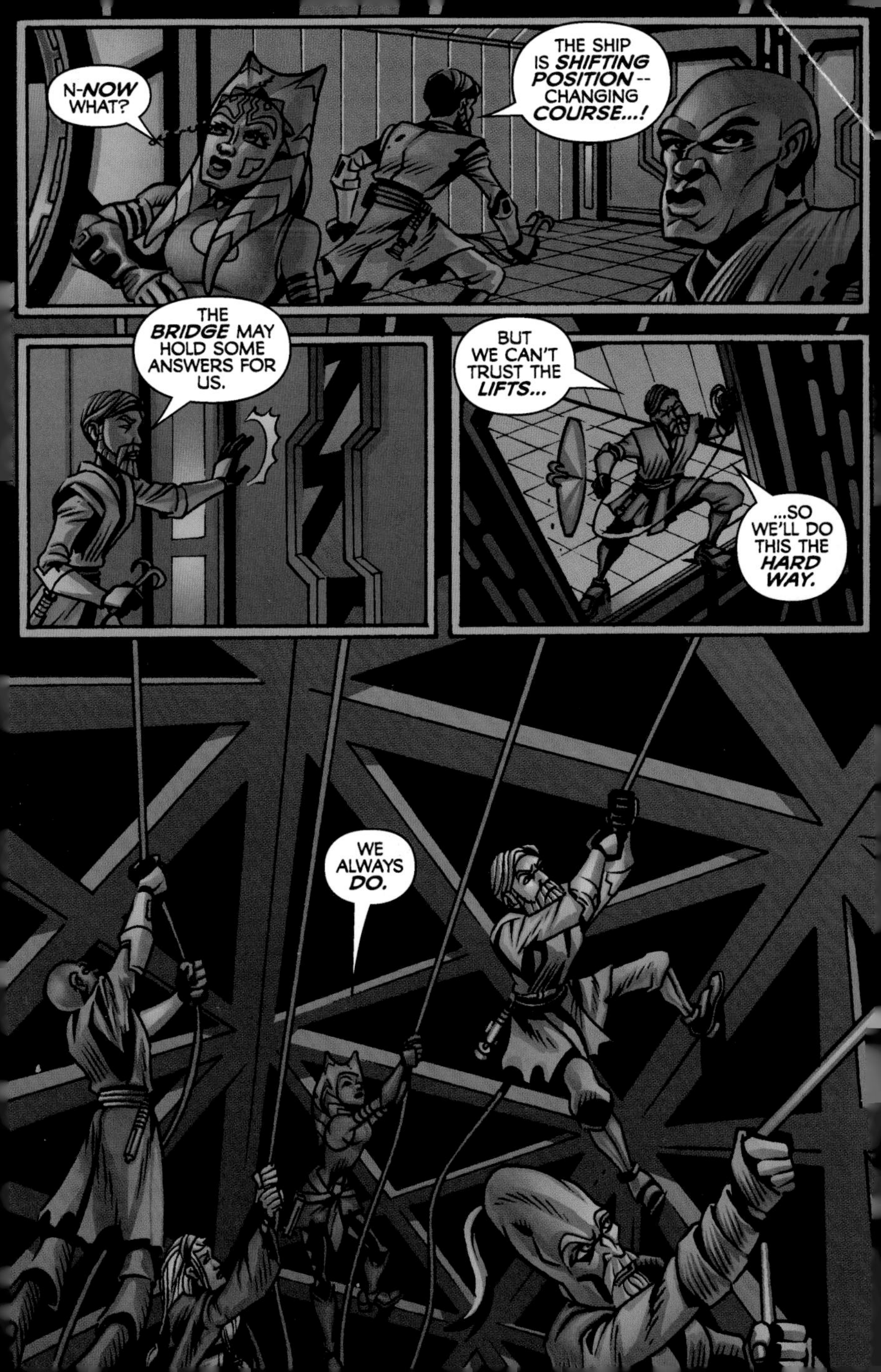
N-NOW WHAT?
THE SHIP IS SHIFTING POSITION -- CHANGING COURSE...!
THE BRIDGE MAY HOLD SOME ANSWERS FOR US.
BUT WE CAN'T TRUST THE LIFTS...
...SO WE'LL DO THIS THE HARD WAY.
WE ALWAYS DO.

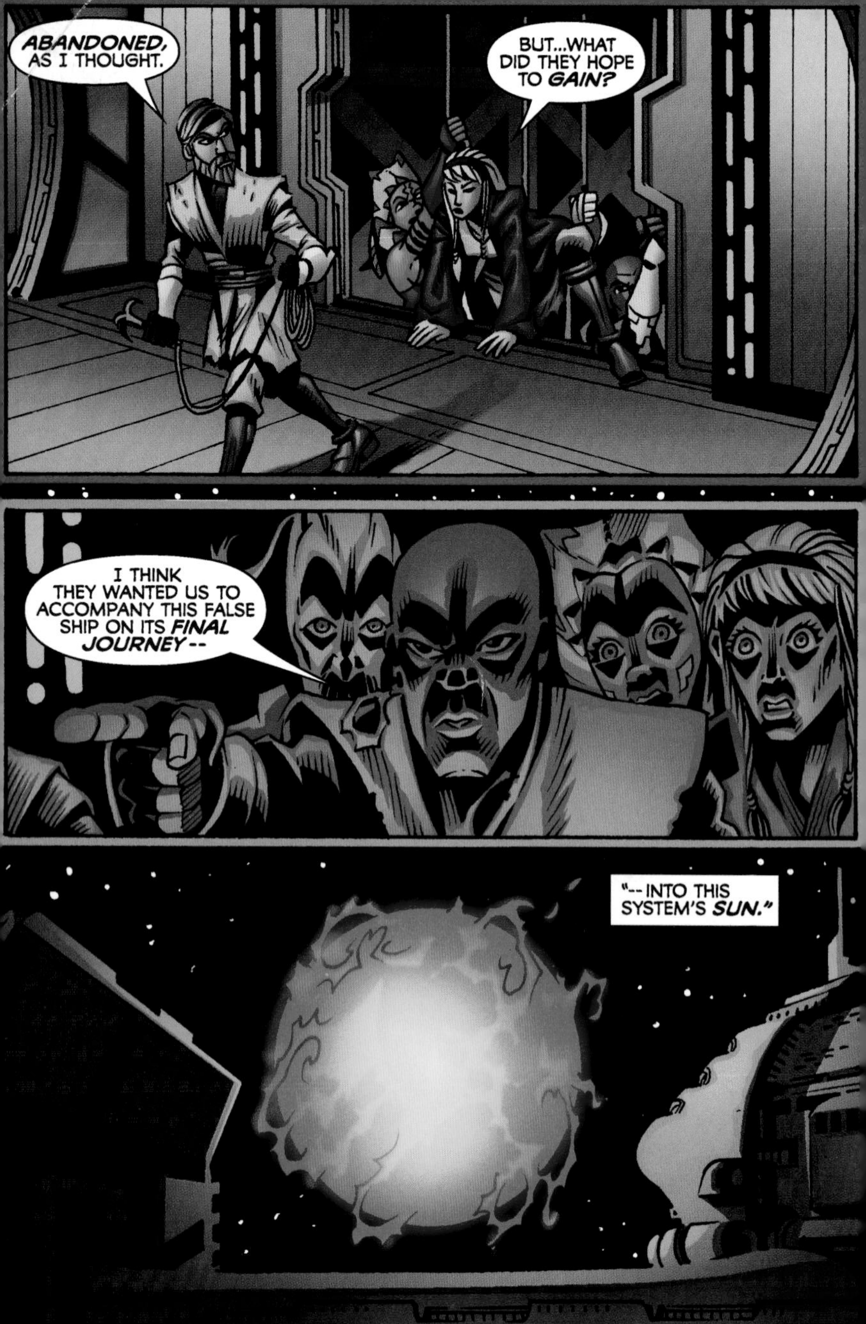
ABANDONED, AS I THOUGHT.
BUT...WHAT DID THEY HOPE TO GAIN?
I THINK THEY WANTED US TO ACCOMPANY THIS FALSE SHIP ON ITS FINAL JOURNEY --
"-- INTO THIS SYSTEM'S SUN."

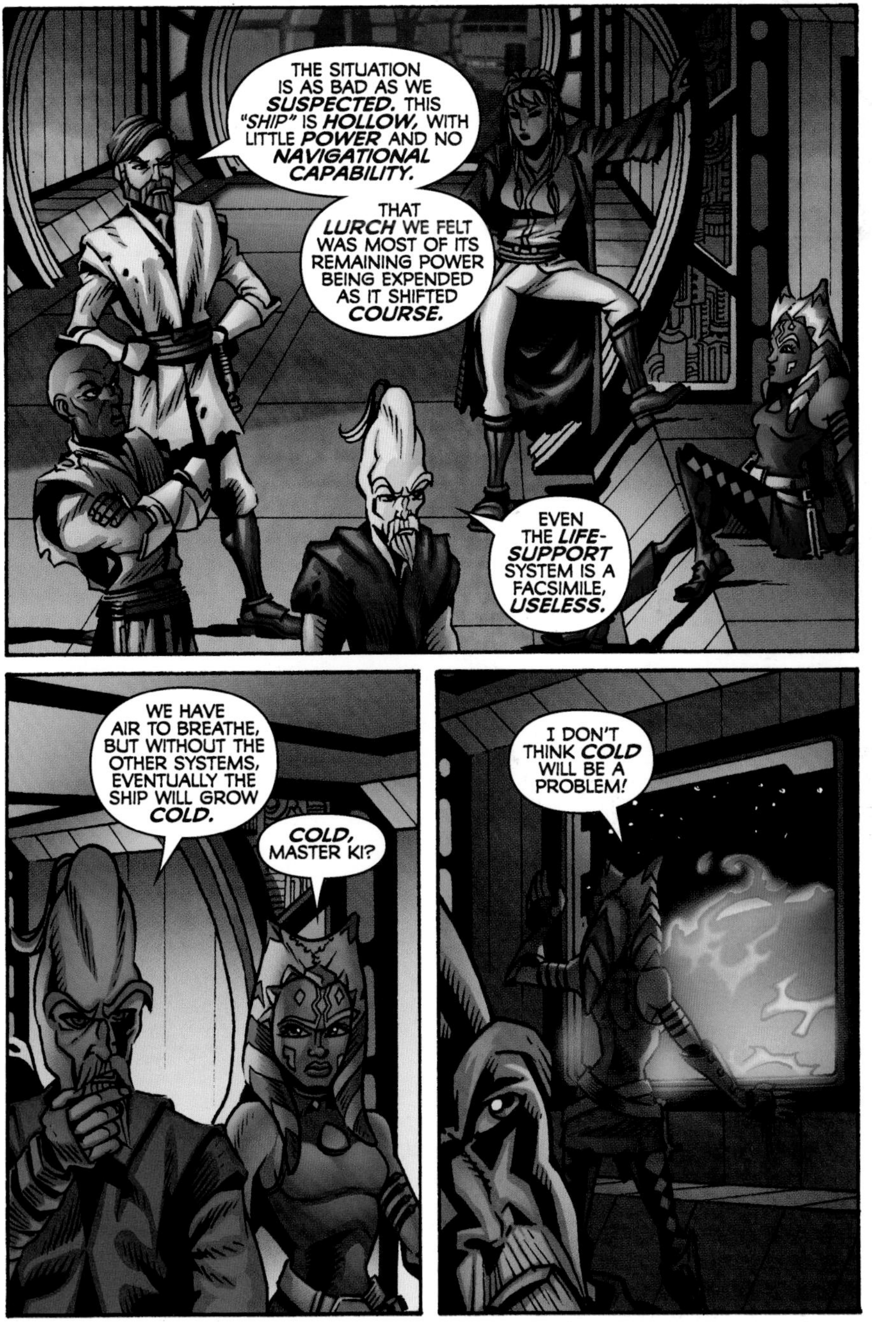
THE SITUATION IS AS BAD AS WE SUSPECTED. THIS "SHIP" IS HOLLOW, WITH LITTLE POWER AND NO NAVIGATIONAL CAPABILITY.
THAT LURCH WE FELT WAS MOST OF ITS REMAINING POWER BEING EXPENDED AS IT SHIFTED COURSE.
EVEN THE LIFE-SUPPORT SYSTEM IS A FACSIMILE, USELESS.
WE HAVE AIR TO BREATHE, BUT WITHOUT THE OTHER SYSTEMS, EVENTUALLY THE SHIP WILL GROW COLD.
COLD, MASTER KI?
I DON'T THINK COLD WILL BE A PROBLEM!

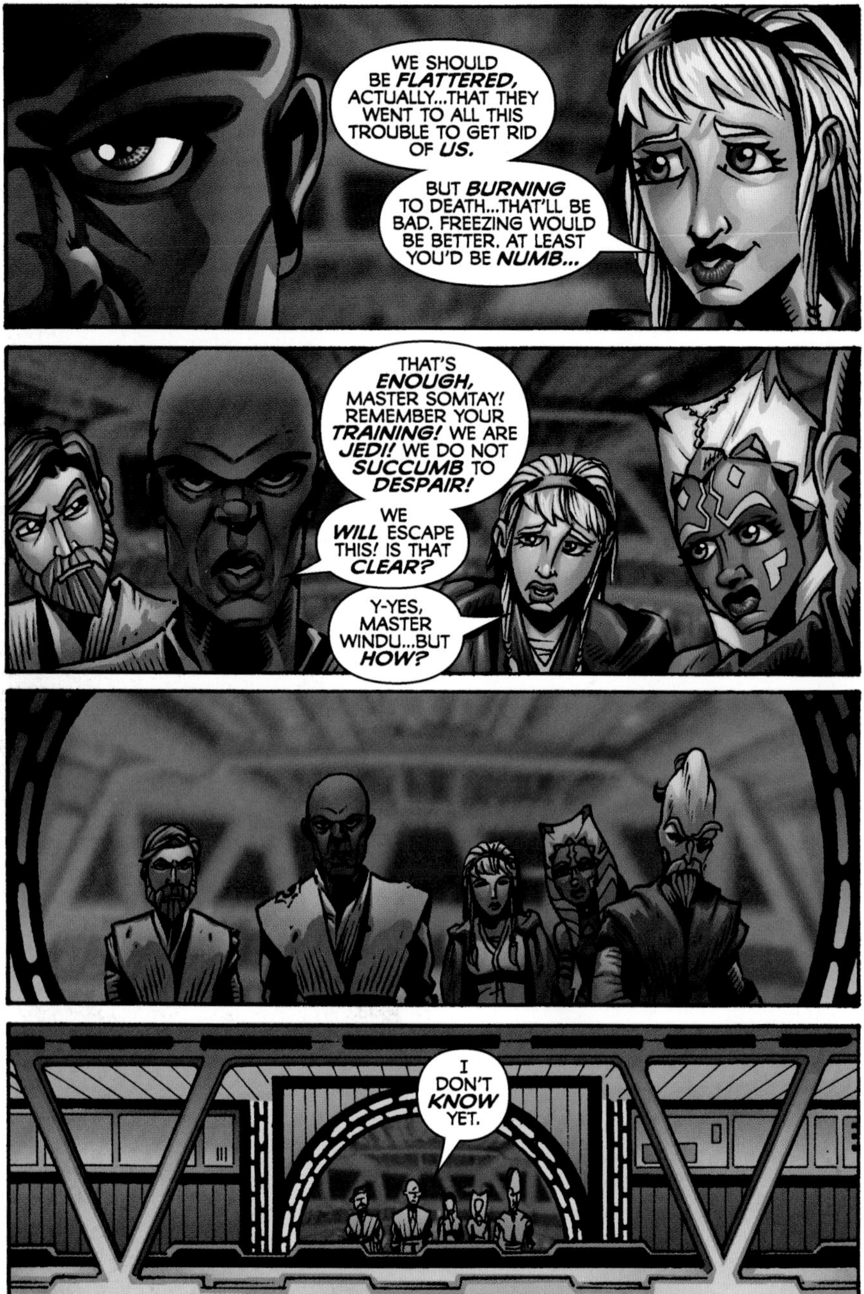
WE SHOULD BE FLATTERED, ACTUALLY...THAT THEY WENT TO ALL THIS TROUBLE TO GET RID OF US.
BUT BURNING TO DEATH...THAT'LL BE BAD. FREEZING WOULD BE BETTER. AT LEAST YOU'D BE NUMB...
THAT'S ENOUGH, MASTER SOMTAY! REMEMBER YOUR TRAINING! WE ARE JEDI! WE DO NOT SUCCUMB TO DESPAIR!
WE WILL ESCAPE THIS! IS THAT CLEAR?
Y-YES, MASTER WINDU...BUT HOW?
I DON'T KNOW YET.

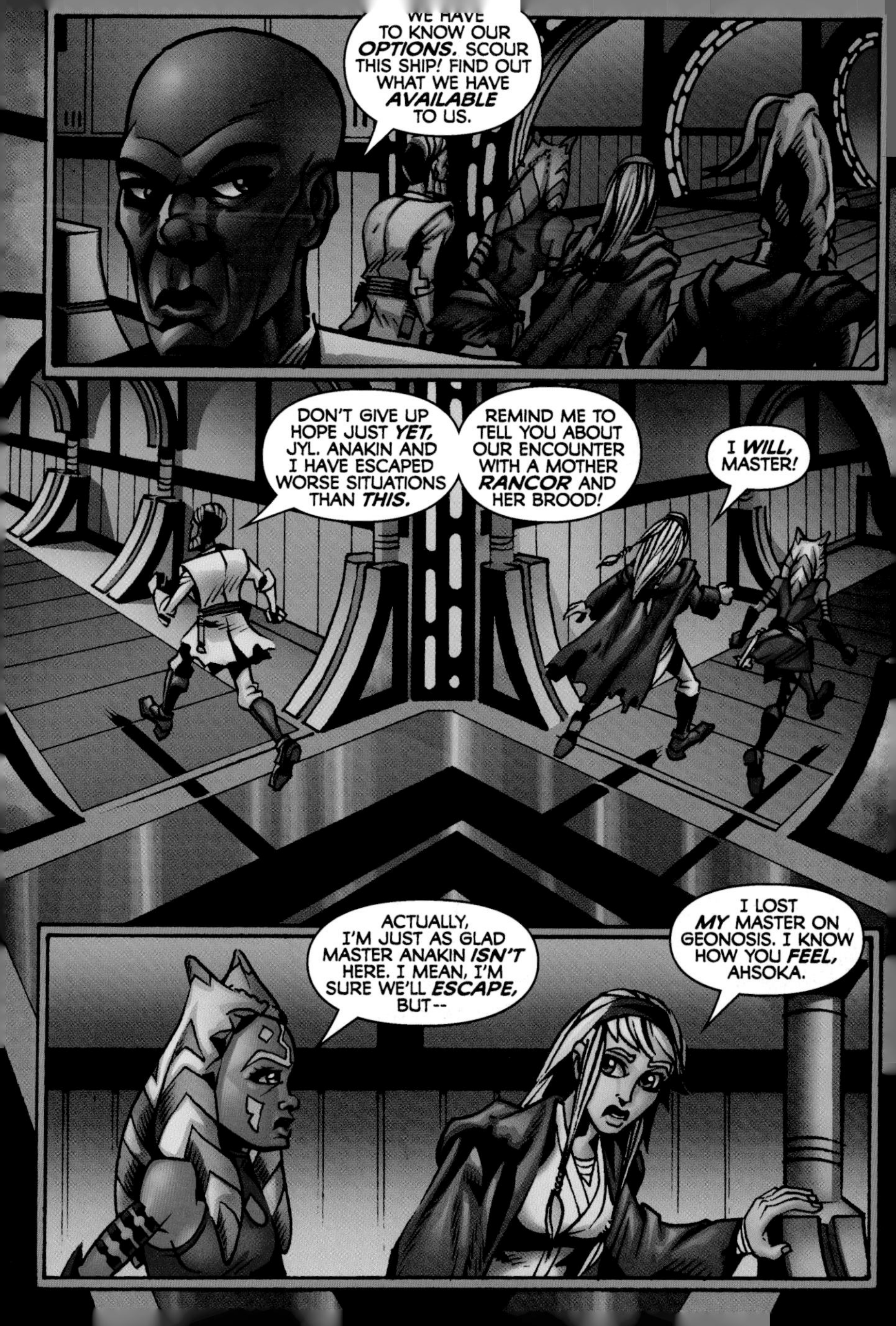

WE HAVE TO KNOW OUR *OPTIONS.* SCOUR THIS SHIP! FIND OUT WHAT WE HAVE *AVAILABLE* TO US.
DON'T GIVE UP HOPE JUST *YET,* JYL. ANAKIN AND I HAVE ESCAPED WORSE SITUATIONS THAN *THIS.*
REMIND ME TO TELL YOU ABOUT OUR ENCOUNTER WITH A MOTHER *RANCOR* AND HER BROOD!
I *WILL,* MASTER!
ACTUALLY, I'M JUST AS GLAD MASTER ANAKIN *ISN'T* HERE. I MEAN, I'M SURE WE'LL *ESCAPE,* BUT--
I LOST *MY* MASTER ON GEONOSIS. I KNOW HOW YOU *FEEL,* AHSOKA.

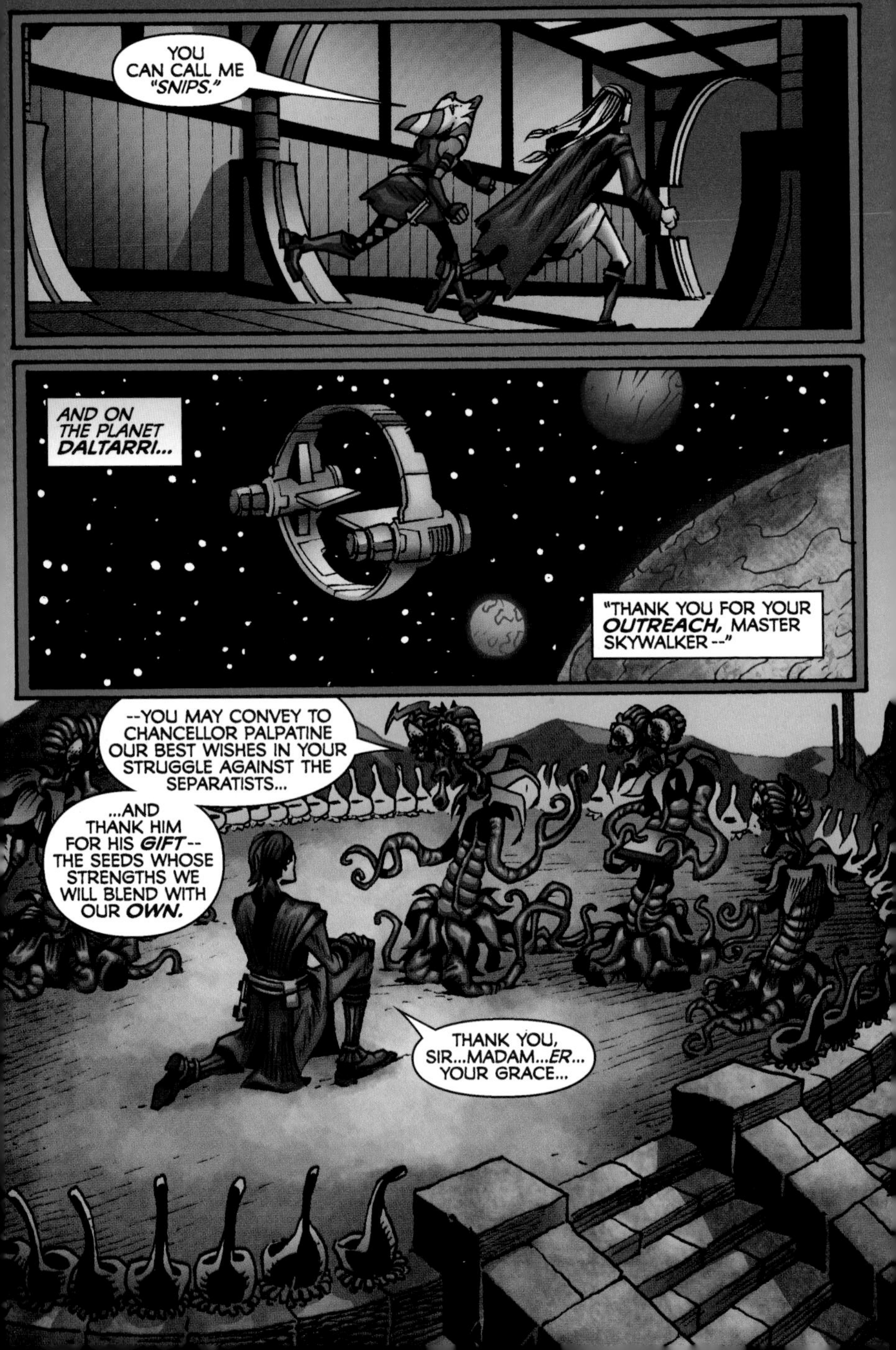
YOU CAN CALL ME "SNIPS."
AND ON THE PLANET DALTARRI...
"THANK YOU FOR YOUR OUTREACH, MASTER SKYWALKER--"
--YOU MAY CONVEY TO CHANCELLOR PALPATINE OUR BEST WISHES IN YOUR STRUGGLE AGAINST THE SEPARATISTS...
...AND THANK HIM FOR HIS GIFT-- THE SEEDS WHOSE STRENGTHS WE WILL BLEND WITH OUR OWN.
THANK YOU, SIR...MADAM...ER... YOUR GRACE...

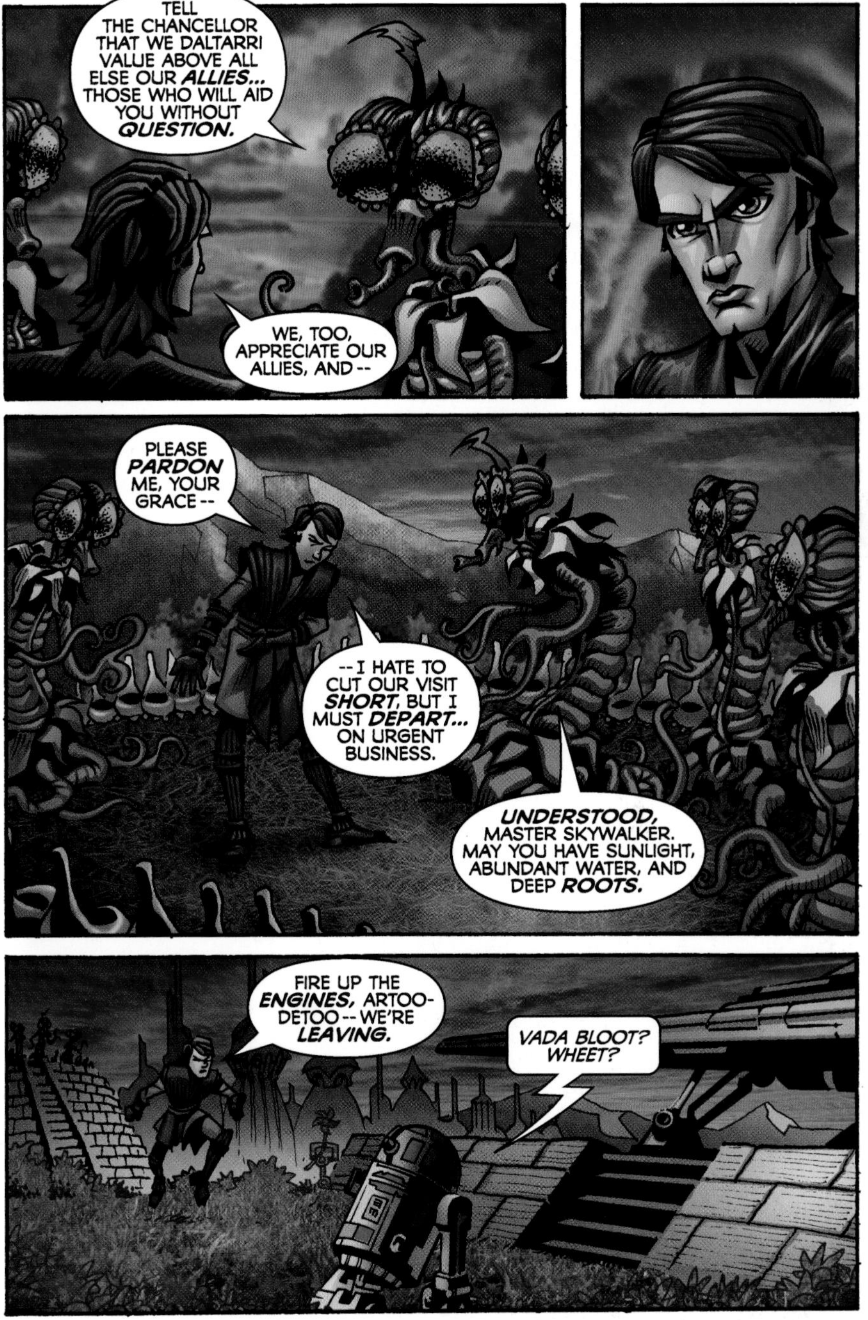

TELL THE CHANCELLOR THAT WE DALTARRI VALUE ABOVE ALL ELSE OUR ALLIES... THOSE WHO WILL AID YOU WITHOUT QUESTION.
WE, TOO, APPRECIATE OUR ALLIES, AND --
PLEASE PARDON ME, YOUR GRACE --
-- I HATE TO CUT OUR VISIT SHORT, BUT I MUST DEPART... ON URGENT BUSINESS.
UNDERSTOOD, MASTER SKYWALKER. MAY YOU HAVE SUNLIGHT, ABUNDANT WATER, AND DEEP ROOTS.
FIRE UP THE ENGINES, ARTOO-DETOO -- WE'RE LEAVING.
VADA BLOOT? WHEET?

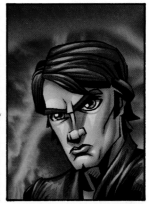

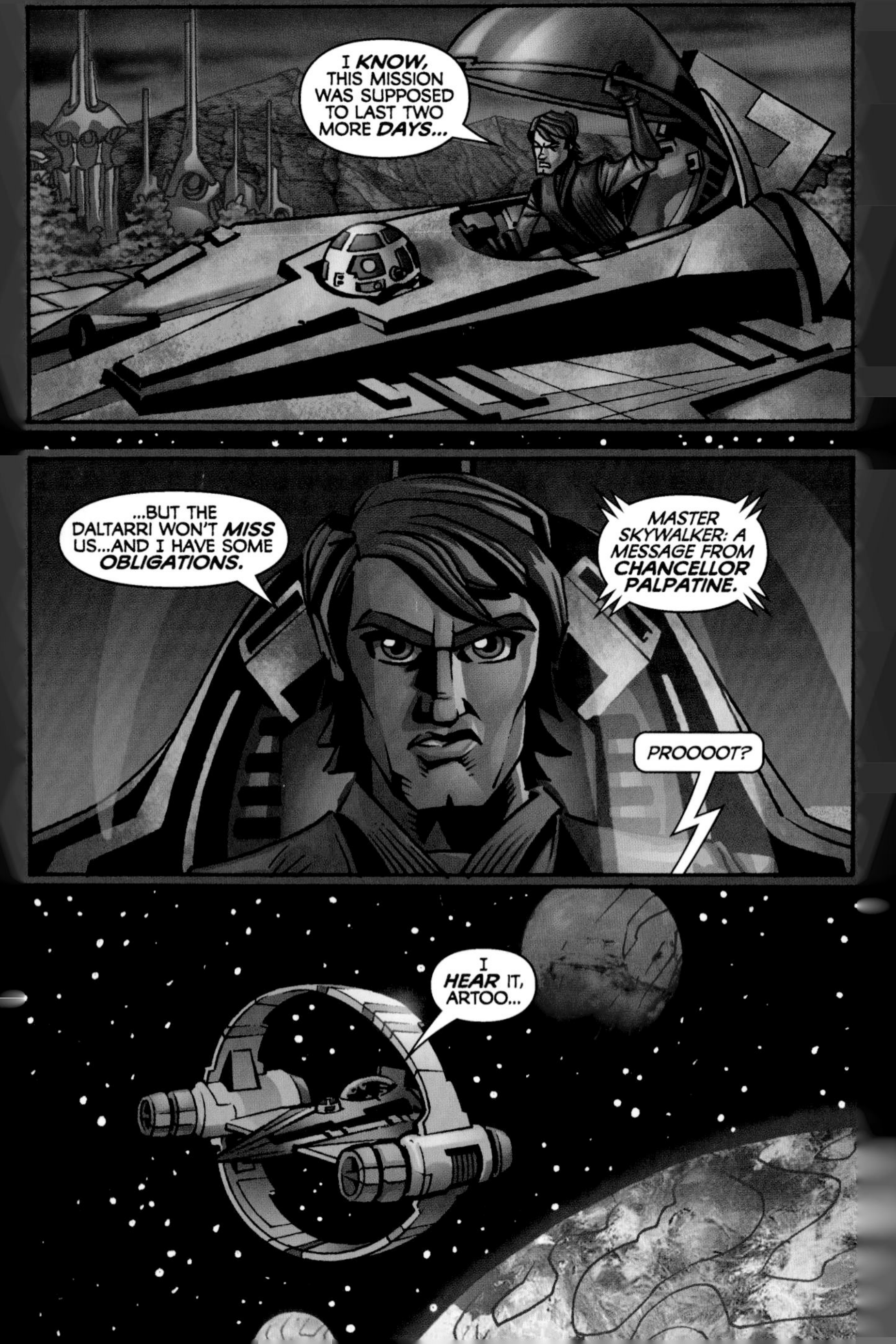
I KNOW, THIS MISSION WAS SUPPOSED TO LAST TWO MORE DAYS...
...BUT THE DALTARRI WON'T MISS US...AND I HAVE SOME OBLIGATIONS.
MASTER SKYWALKER: A MESSAGE FROM CHANCELLOR PALPATINE.
PROOOOT?
I HEAR IT, ARTOO...

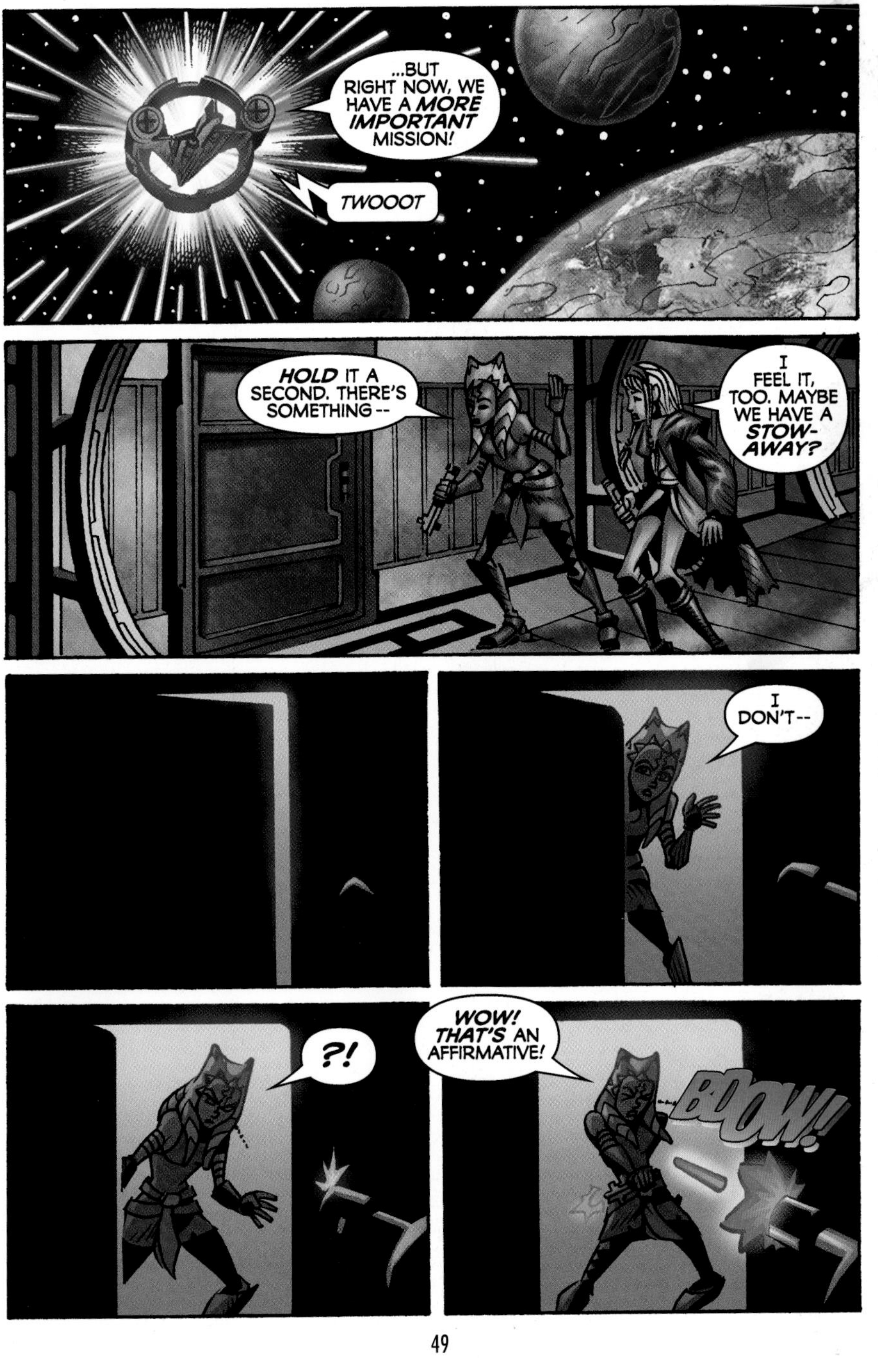
...BUT RIGHT NOW, WE HAVE A *MORE IMPORTANT* MISSION!
TWOOOT
HOLD IT A SECOND. THERE'S SOMETHING --
I FEEL IT, TOO. MAYBE WE HAVE A *STOW-AWAY?*
I DON'T --
?!
WOW! THAT'S AN AFFIRMATIVE!
BOOW!!

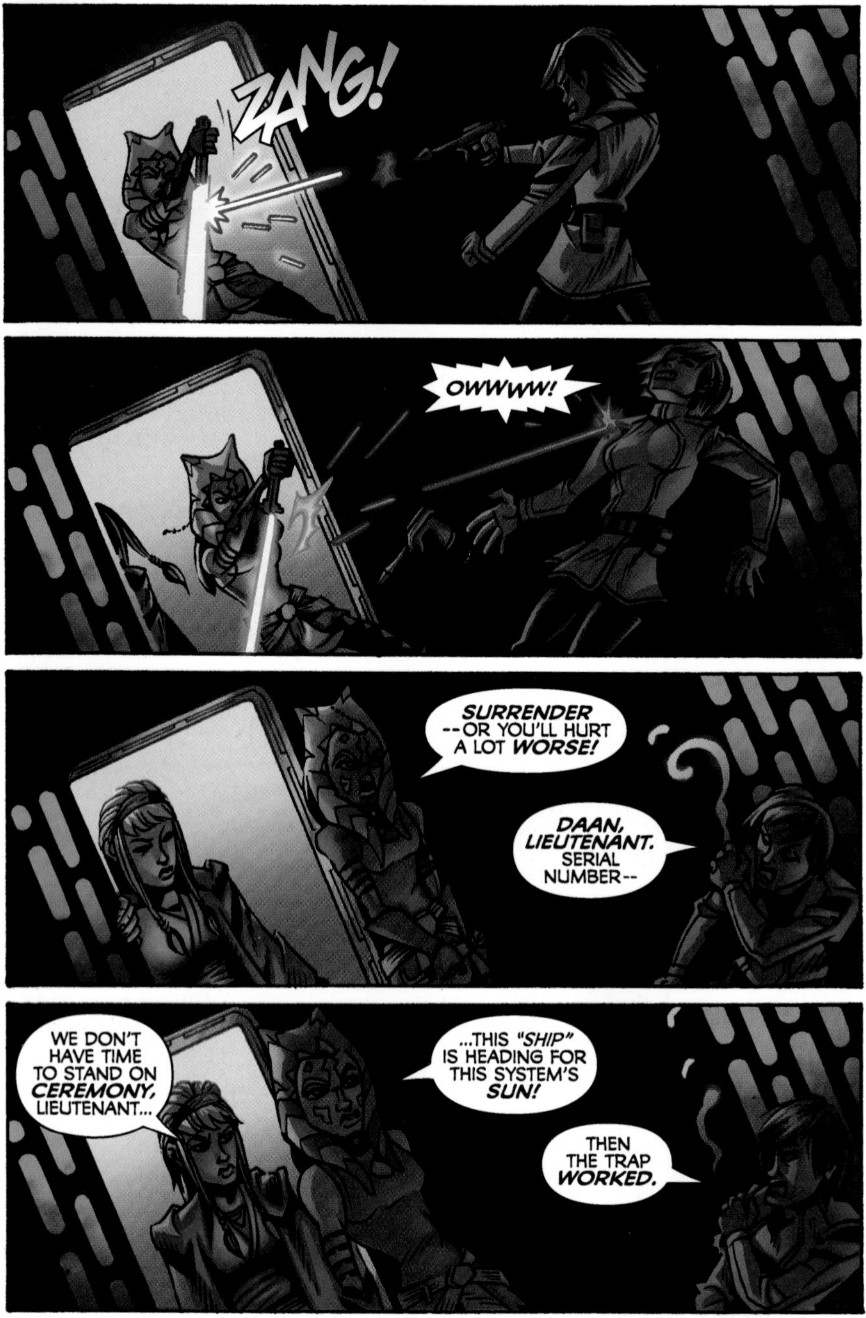
ZANG!
OWWWW!
SURRENDER --OR YOU'LL HURT A LOT WORSE!
DAAN, LIEUTENANT. SERIAL NUMBER--
WE DON'T HAVE TIME TO STAND ON CEREMONY, LIEUTENANT...
...THIS "SHIP" IS HEADING FOR THIS SYSTEM'S SUN!
THEN THE TRAP WORKED.

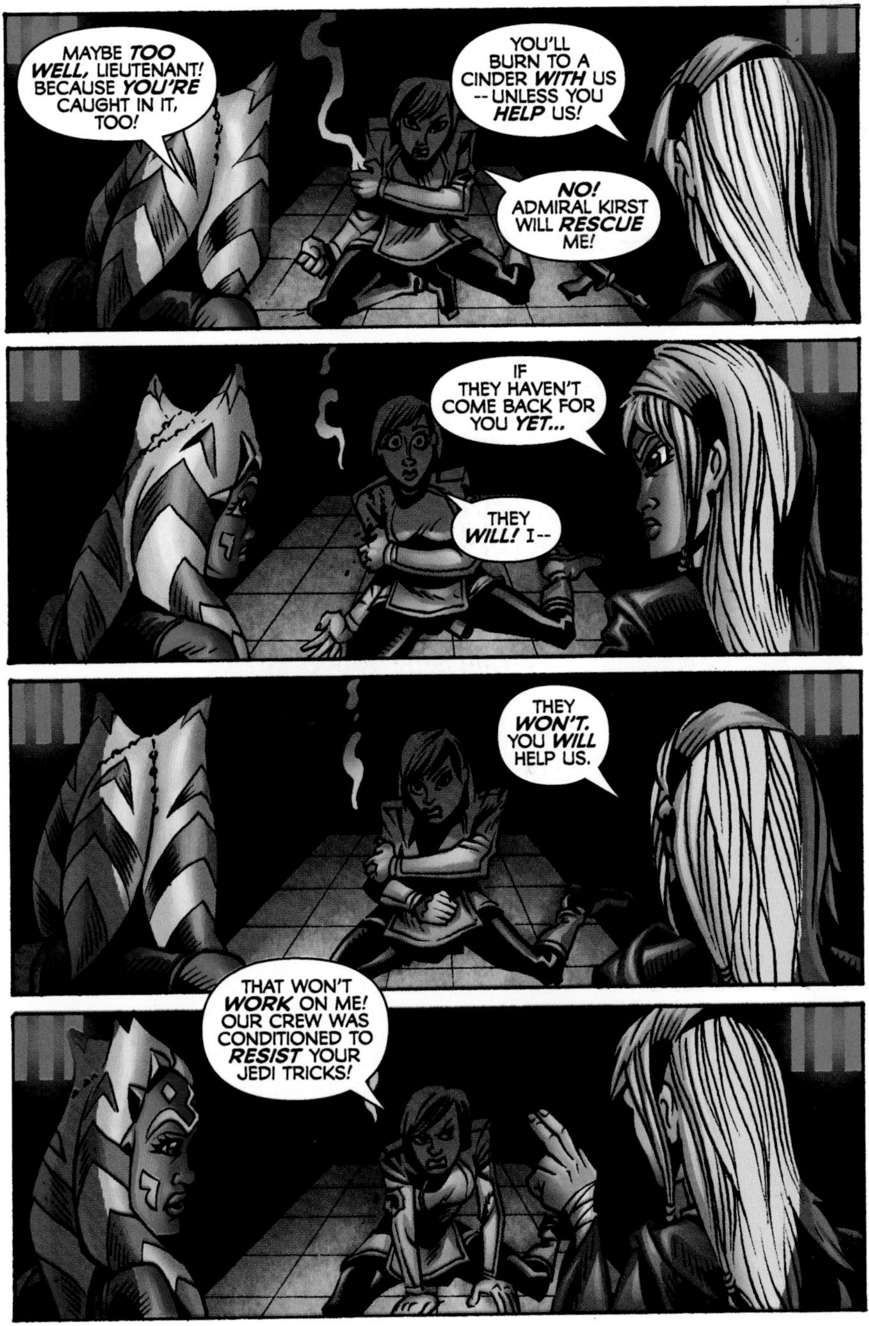
MAYBE TOO WELL, LIEUTENANT! BECAUSE YOU'RE CAUGHT IN IT, TOO!
YOU'LL BURN TO A CINDER WITH US --UNLESS YOU HELP US!
NO! ADMIRAL KIRST WILL RESCUE ME!
IF THEY HAVEN'T COME BACK FOR YOU YET...
THEY WILL! I--
THEY WON'T. YOU WILL HELP US.
THAT WON'T WORK ON ME! OUR CREW WAS CONDITIONED TO RESIST YOUR JEDI TRICKS!

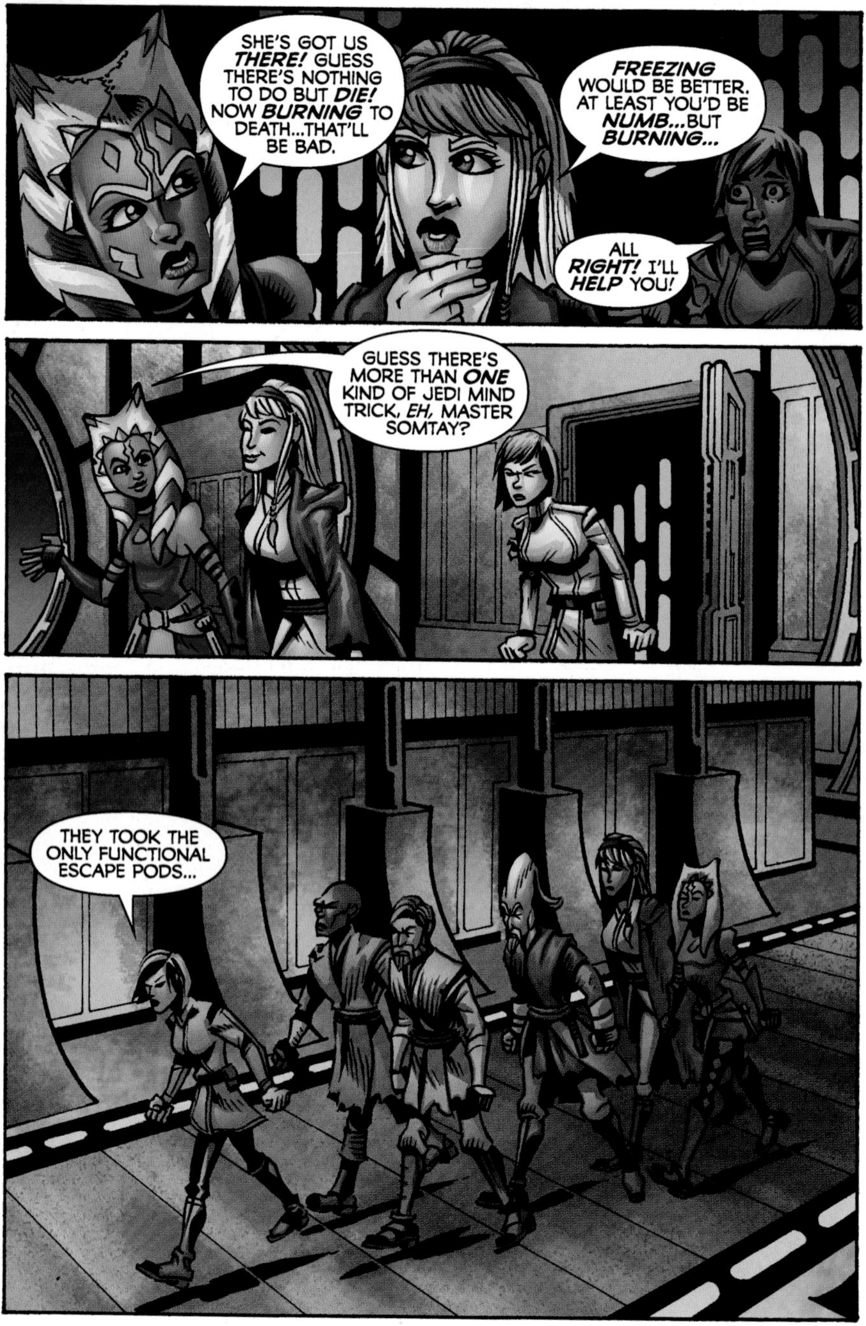
SHE'S GOT US *THERE!* GUESS THERE'S NOTHING TO DO BUT *DIE!* NOW *BURNING* TO DEATH...THAT'LL BE BAD.
FREEZING WOULD BE BETTER. AT LEAST YOU'D BE *NUMB*...BUT *BURNING*...
ALL *RIGHT!* I'LL *HELP* YOU!
GUESS THERE'S MORE THAN *ONE* KIND OF JEDI MIND TRICK, *EH,* MASTER SOMTAY?
THEY TOOK THE ONLY FUNCTIONAL ESCAPE PODS...

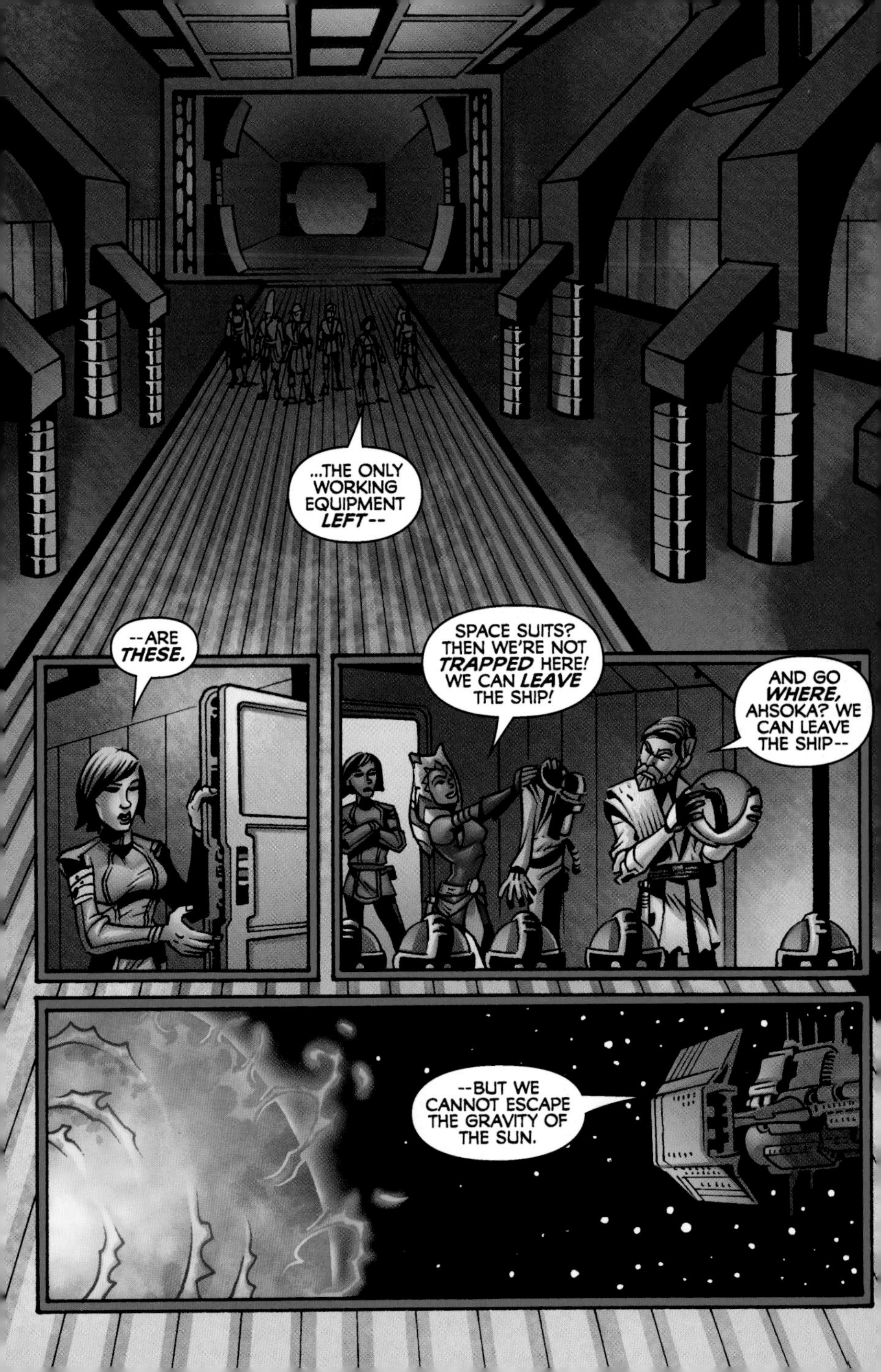
...THE ONLY WORKING EQUIPMENT *LEFT*--
--ARE *THESE.*
SPACE SUITS? THEN WE'RE NOT *TRAPPED* HERE! WE CAN *LEAVE* THE SHIP!
AND GO *WHERE,* AHSOKA? WE CAN LEAVE THE SHIP--
--BUT WE CANNOT ESCAPE THE GRAVITY OF THE SUN.

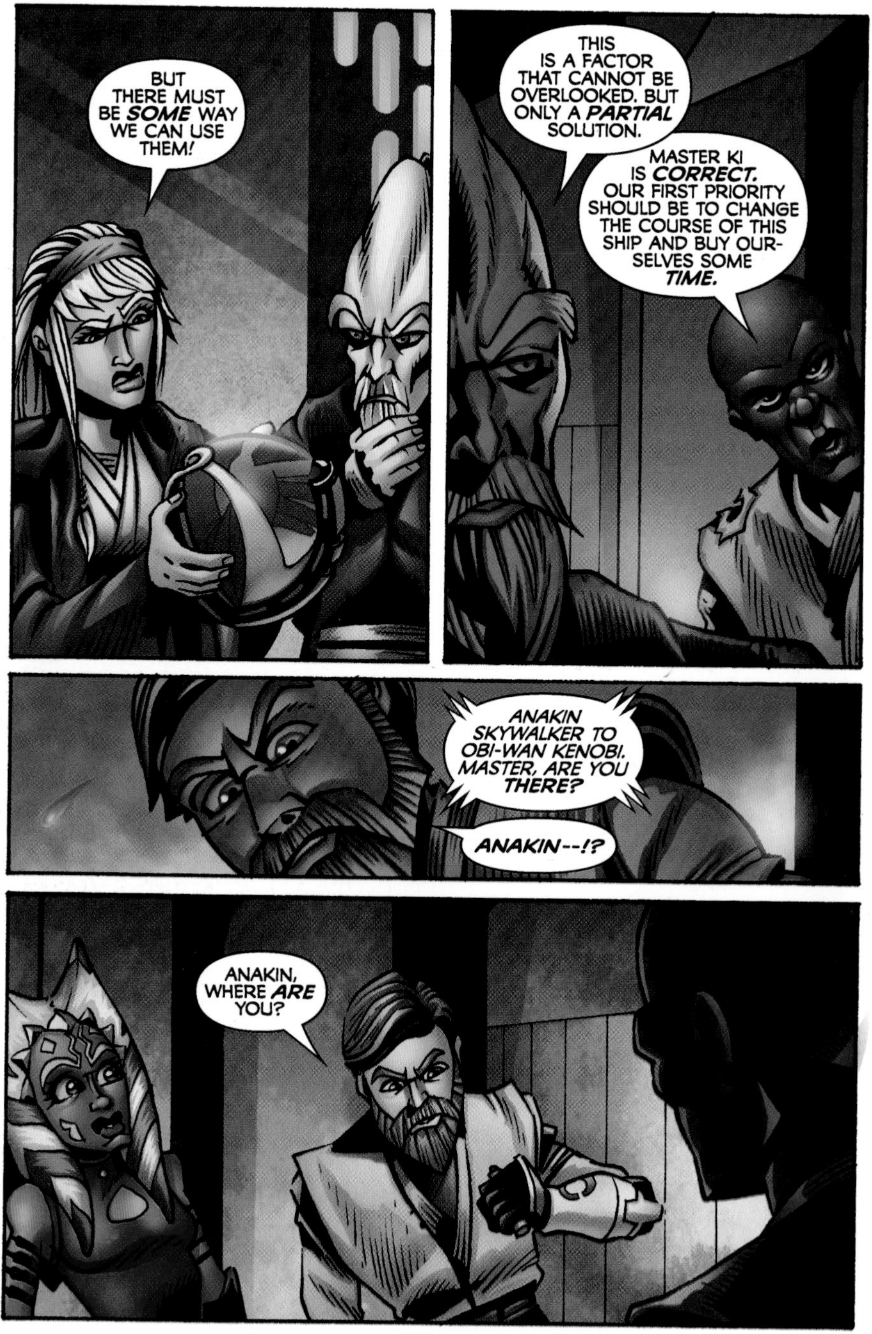
BUT THERE MUST BE SOME WAY WE CAN USE THEM!
THIS IS A FACTOR THAT CANNOT BE OVERLOOKED. BUT ONLY A PARTIAL SOLUTION.
MASTER KI IS CORRECT. OUR FIRST PRIORITY SHOULD BE TO CHANGE THE COURSE OF THIS SHIP AND BUY OURSELVES SOME TIME.
ANAKIN SKYWALKER TO OBI-WAN KENOBI. MASTER, ARE YOU THERE?
ANAKIN--!?
ANAKIN, WHERE ARE YOU?

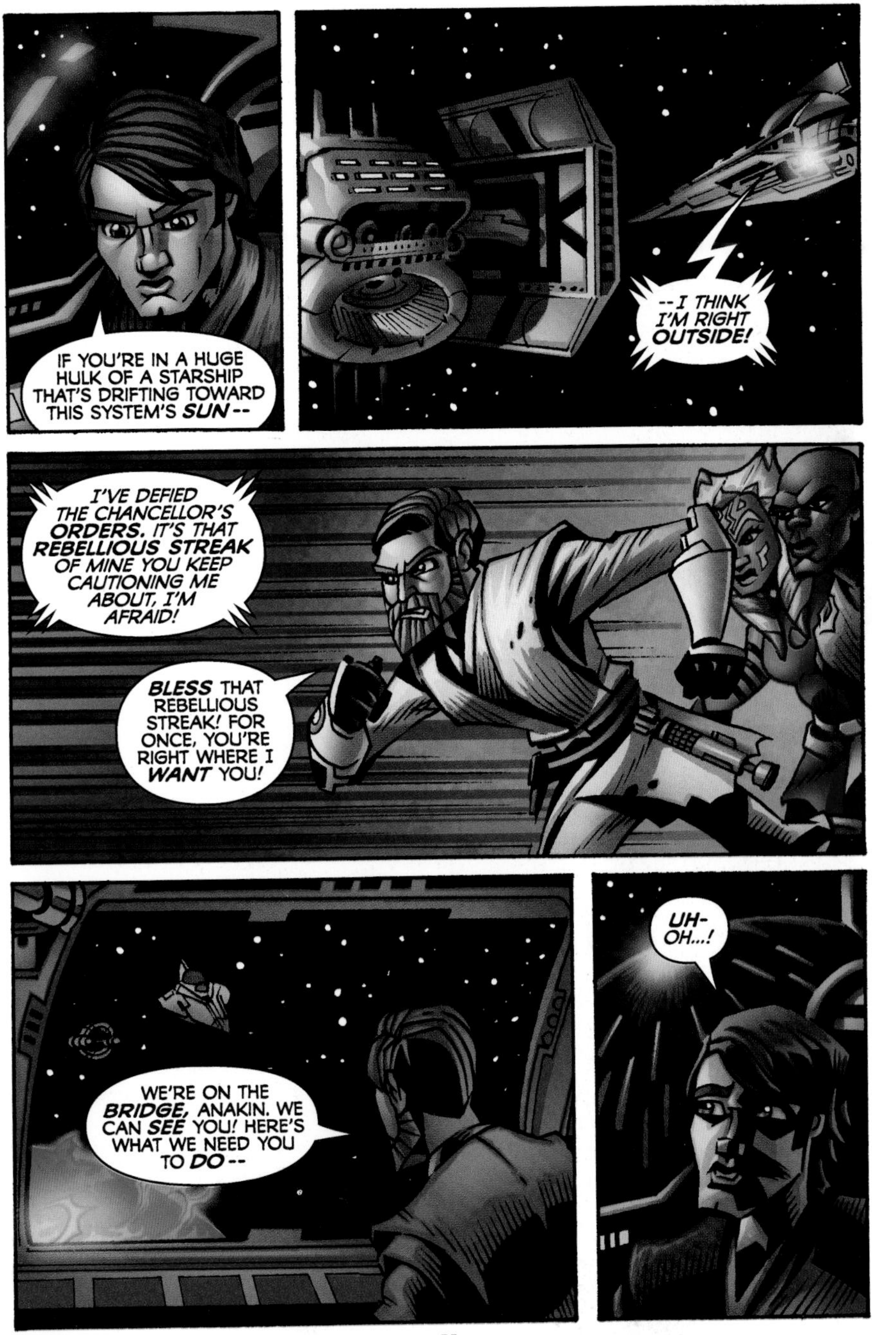
IF YOU'RE IN A HUGE HULK OF A STARSHIP THAT'S DRIFTING TOWARD THIS SYSTEM'S SUN --
-- I THINK I'M RIGHT OUTSIDE!
I'VE DEFIED THE CHANCELLOR'S ORDERS. IT'S THAT REBELLIOUS STREAK OF MINE YOU KEEP CAUTIONING ME ABOUT, I'M AFRAID!
BLESS THAT REBELLIOUS STREAK! FOR ONCE, YOU'RE RIGHT WHERE I WANT YOU!
WE'RE ON THE BRIDGE, ANAKIN. WE CAN SEE YOU! HERE'S WHAT WE NEED YOU TO DO --
UH-OH...!

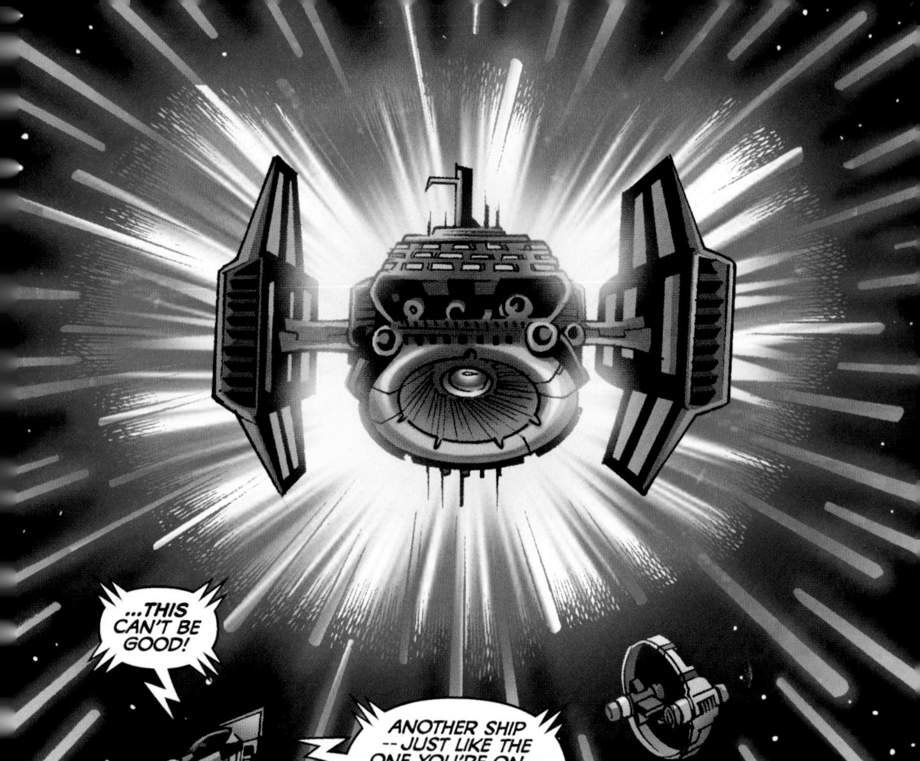
...THIS CAN'T BE GOOD!
ANOTHER SHIP --JUST LIKE THE ONE YOU'RE ON-- HAS ARRIVED. ONLY THIS ONE'S ENERGY READINGS ARE AT THE TOP OF THE GAUGE!

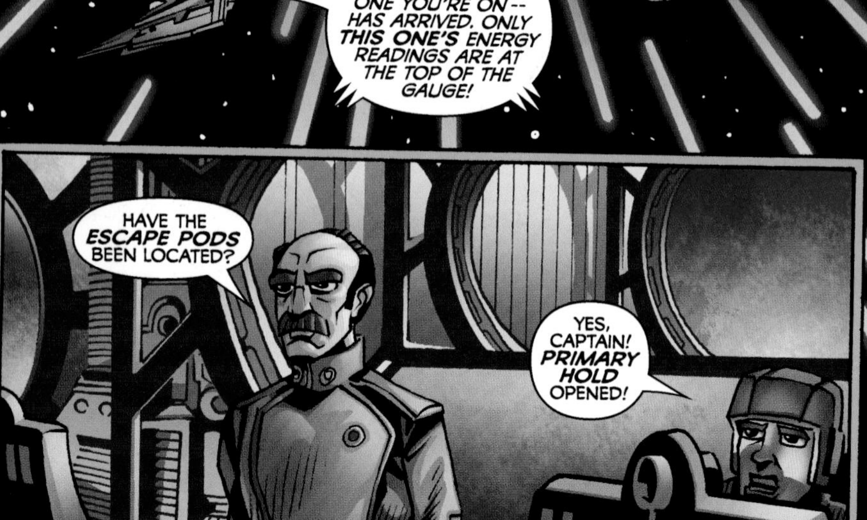
HAVE THE ESCAPE PODS BEEN LOCATED?
YES, CAPTAIN! PRIMARY HOLD OPENED!

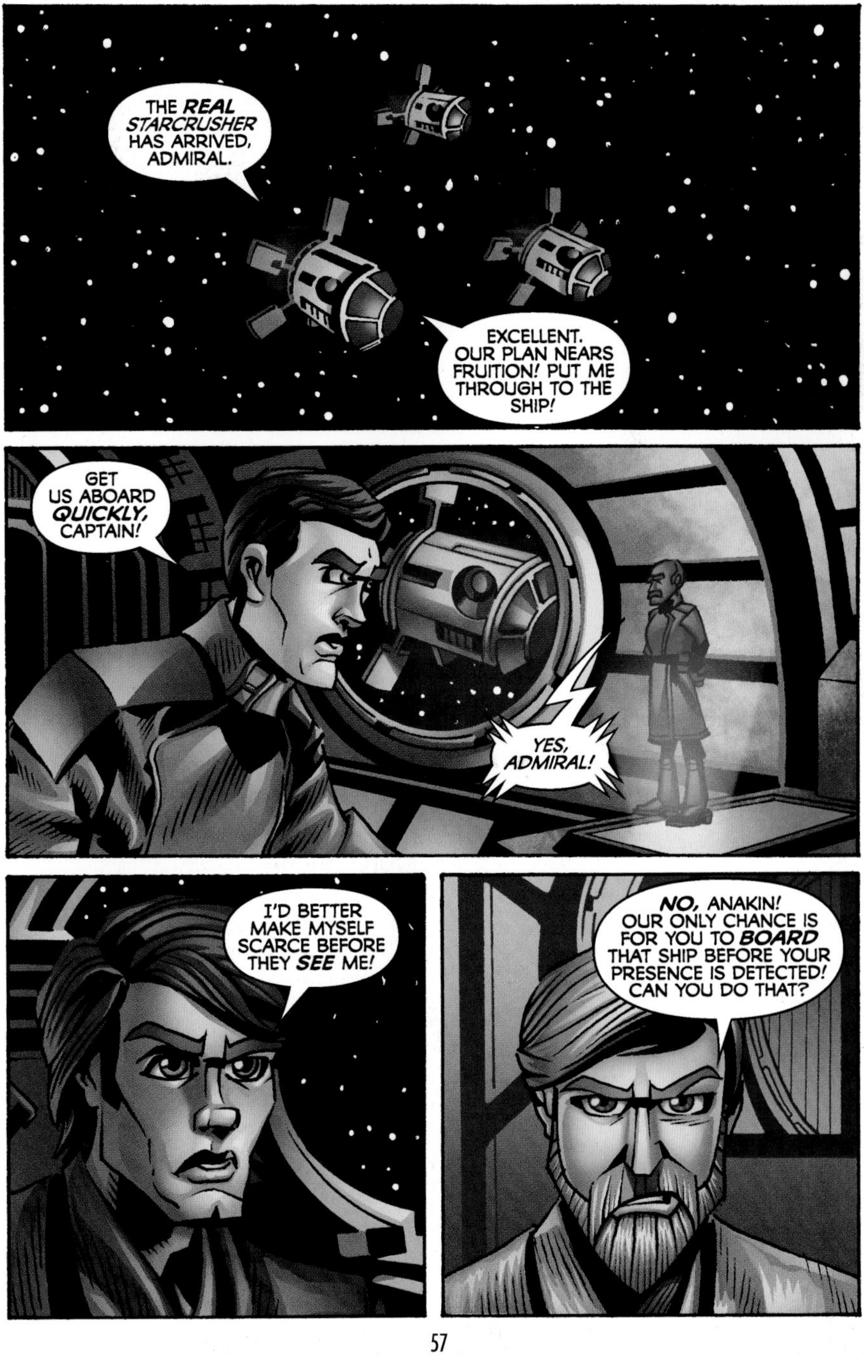
THE REAL STARCRUSHER HAS ARRIVED, ADMIRAL.
EXCELLENT. OUR PLAN NEARS FRUITION! PUT ME THROUGH TO THE SHIP!
GET US ABOARD QUICKLY, CAPTAIN!
YES, ADMIRAL!
I'D BETTER MAKE MYSELF SCARCE BEFORE THEY SEE ME!
NO, ANAKIN! OUR ONLY CHANCE IS FOR YOU TO BOARD THAT SHIP BEFORE YOUR PRESENCE IS DETECTED! CAN YOU DO THAT?

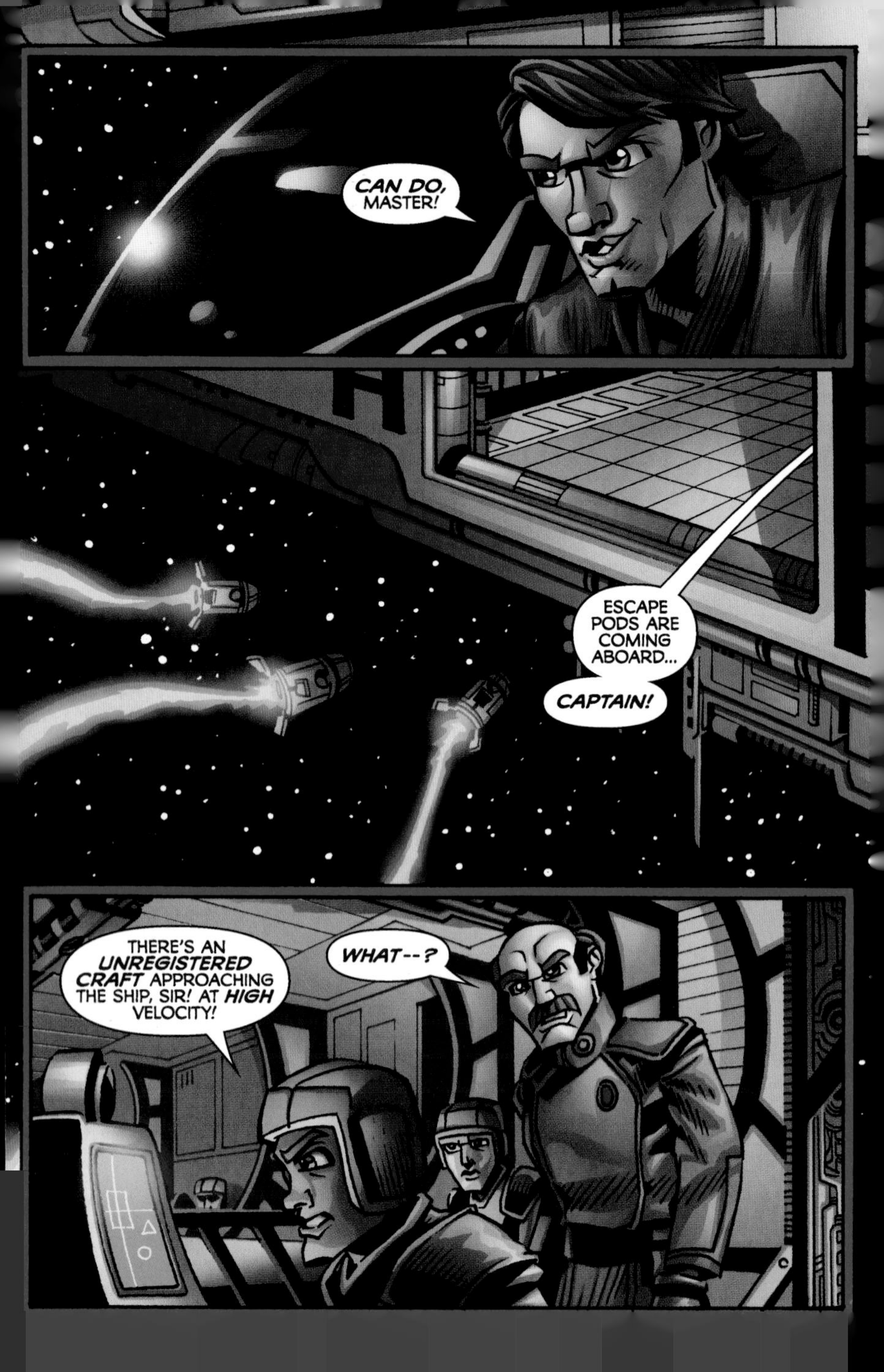
CAN DO, MASTER!
ESCAPE PODS ARE COMING ABOARD...
CAPTAIN!
THERE'S AN UNREGISTERED CRAFT APPROACHING THE SHIP, SIR! AT HIGH VELOCITY!
WHAT--?

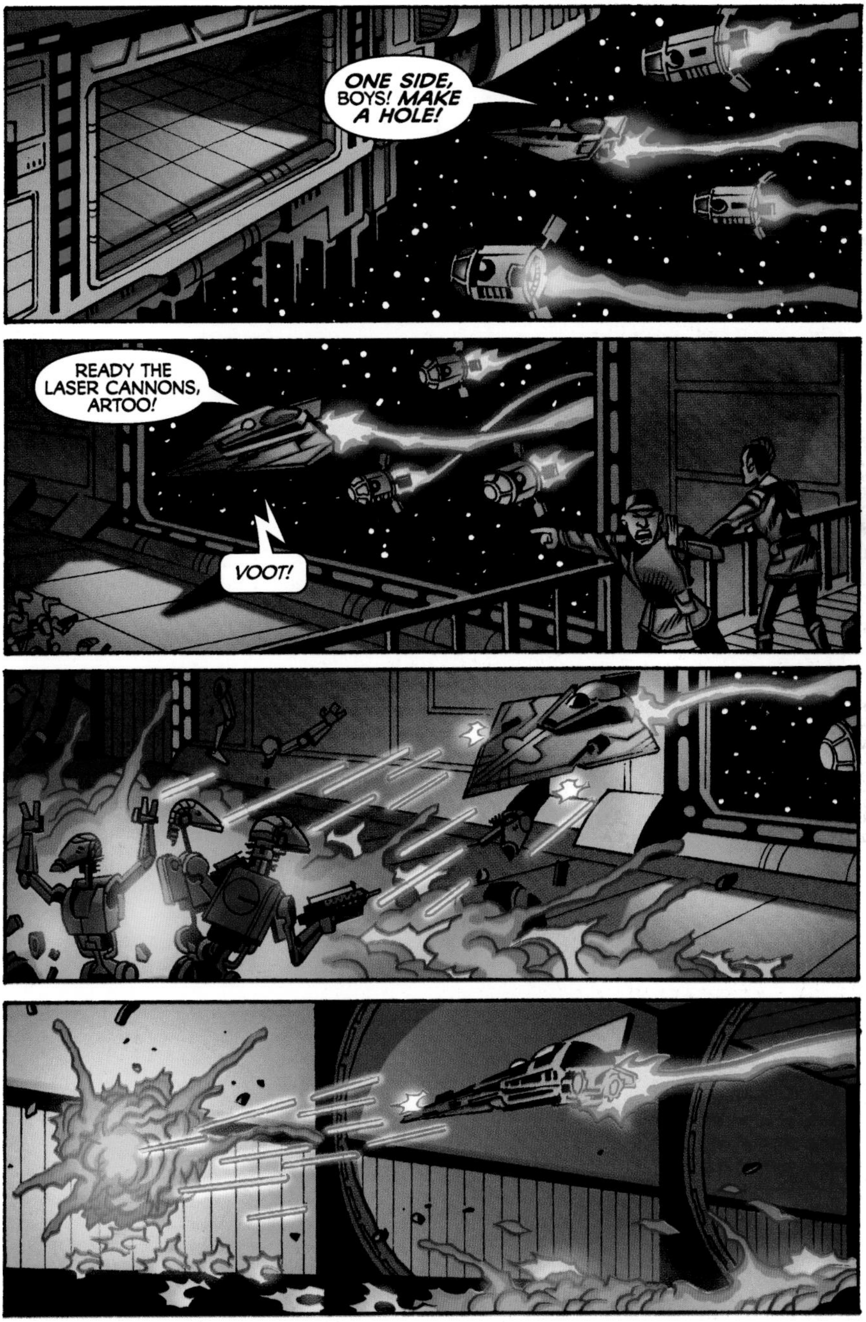
ONE SIDE, BOYS! MAKE A HOLE!
READY THE LASER CANNONS, ARTOO!
VOOT!

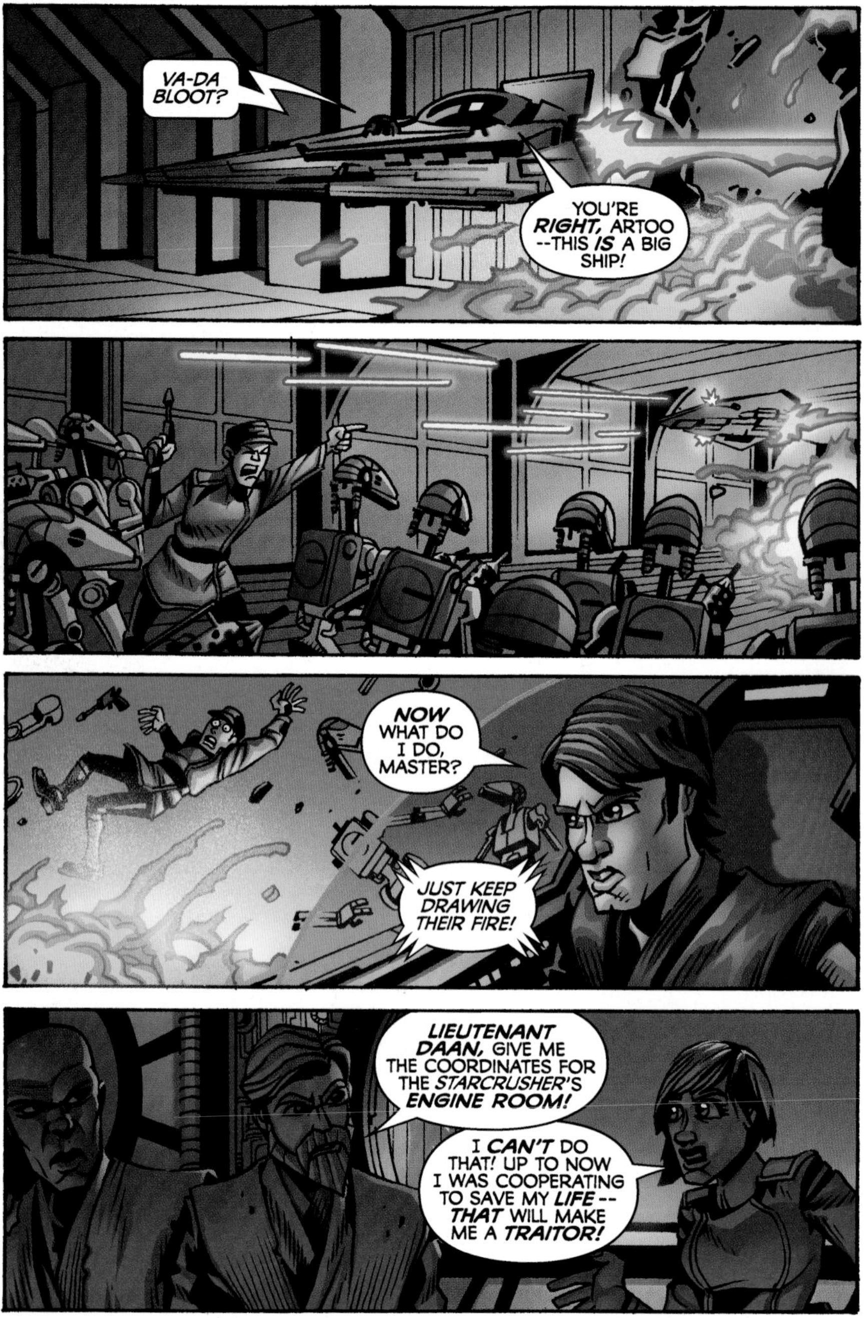
VA-DA BLOOT?
YOU'RE RIGHT, ARTOO --THIS IS A BIG SHIP!
NOW WHAT DO I DO, MASTER?
JUST KEEP DRAWING THEIR FIRE!
LIEUTENANT DAAN, GIVE ME THE COORDINATES FOR THE STARCRUSHER'S ENGINE ROOM!
I CAN'T DO THAT! UP TO NOW I WAS COOPERATING TO SAVE MY LIFE -- THAT WILL MAKE ME A TRAITOR!

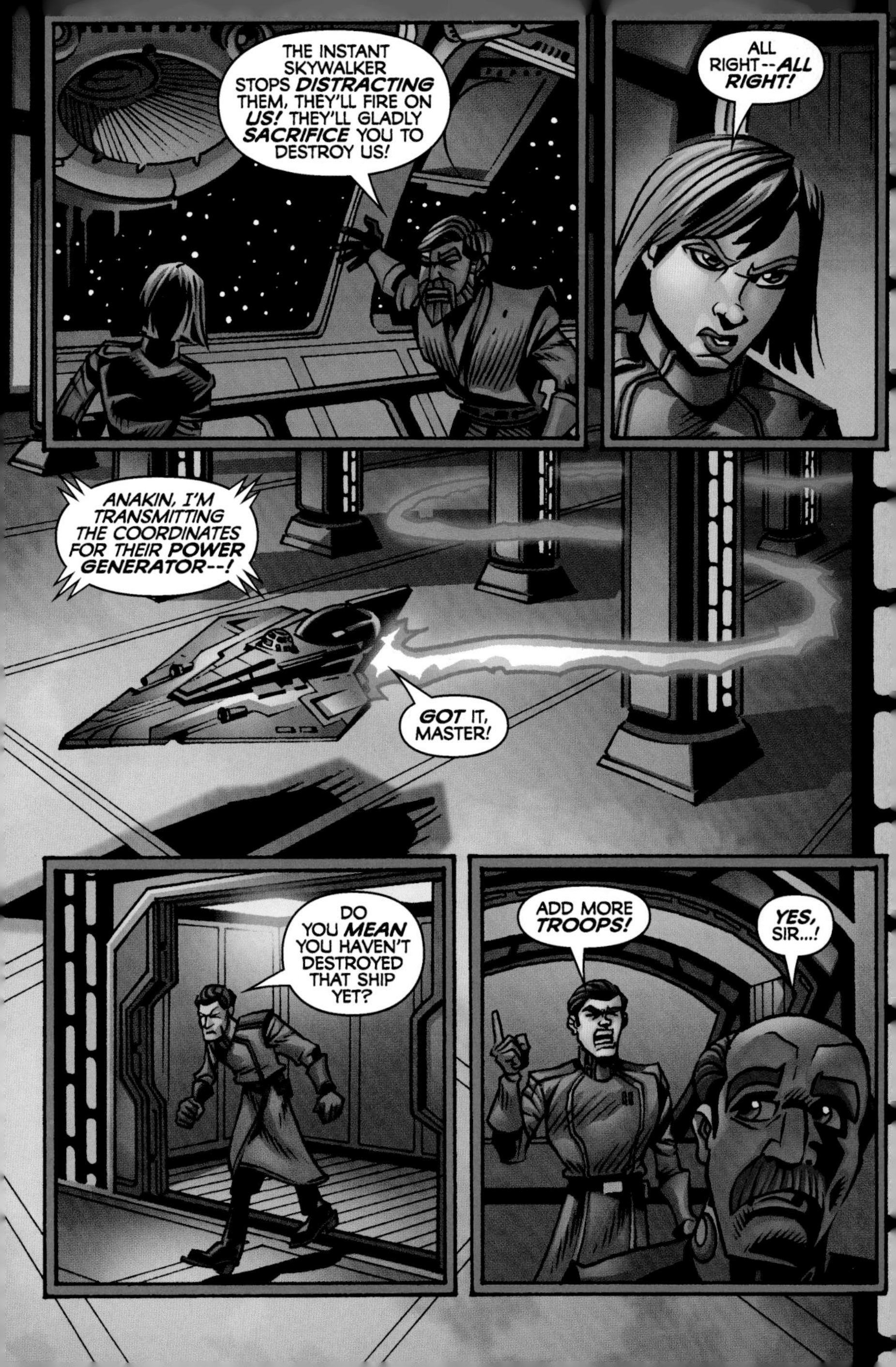
THE INSTANT SKYWALKER STOPS DISTRACTING THEM, THEY'LL FIRE ON US! THEY'LL GLADLY SACRIFICE YOU TO DESTROY US!
ALL RIGHT--ALL RIGHT!
ANAKIN, I'M TRANSMITTING THE COORDINATES FOR THEIR POWER GENERATOR--!
GOT IT, MASTER!
DO YOU MEAN YOU HAVEN'T DESTROYED THAT SHIP YET?
ADD MORE TROOPS!
YES, SIR...!

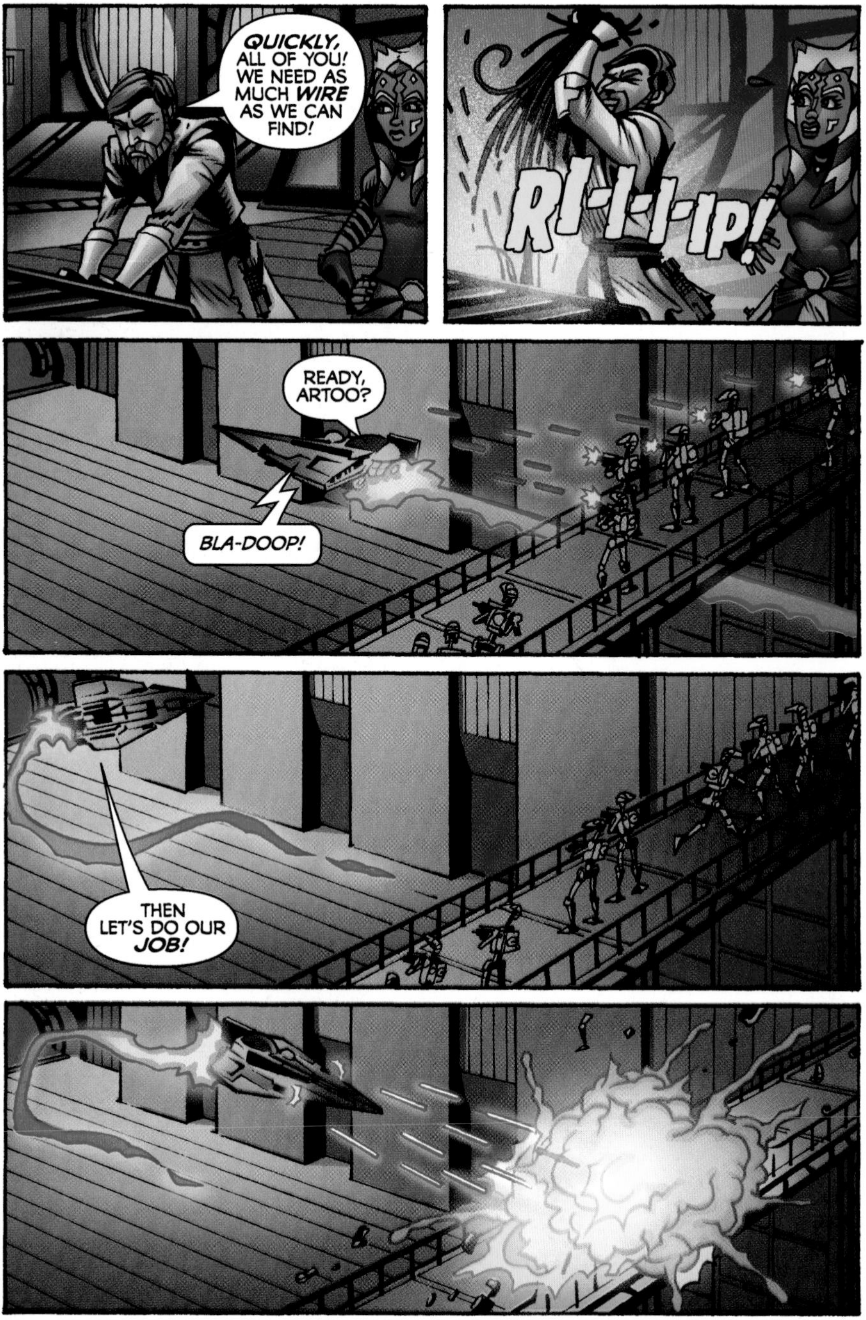
QUICKLY, ALL OF YOU! WE NEED AS MUCH WIRE AS WE CAN FIND!
RI-I-I-IP!
READY, ARTOO?
BLA-DOOP!
THEN LET'S DO OUR JOB!

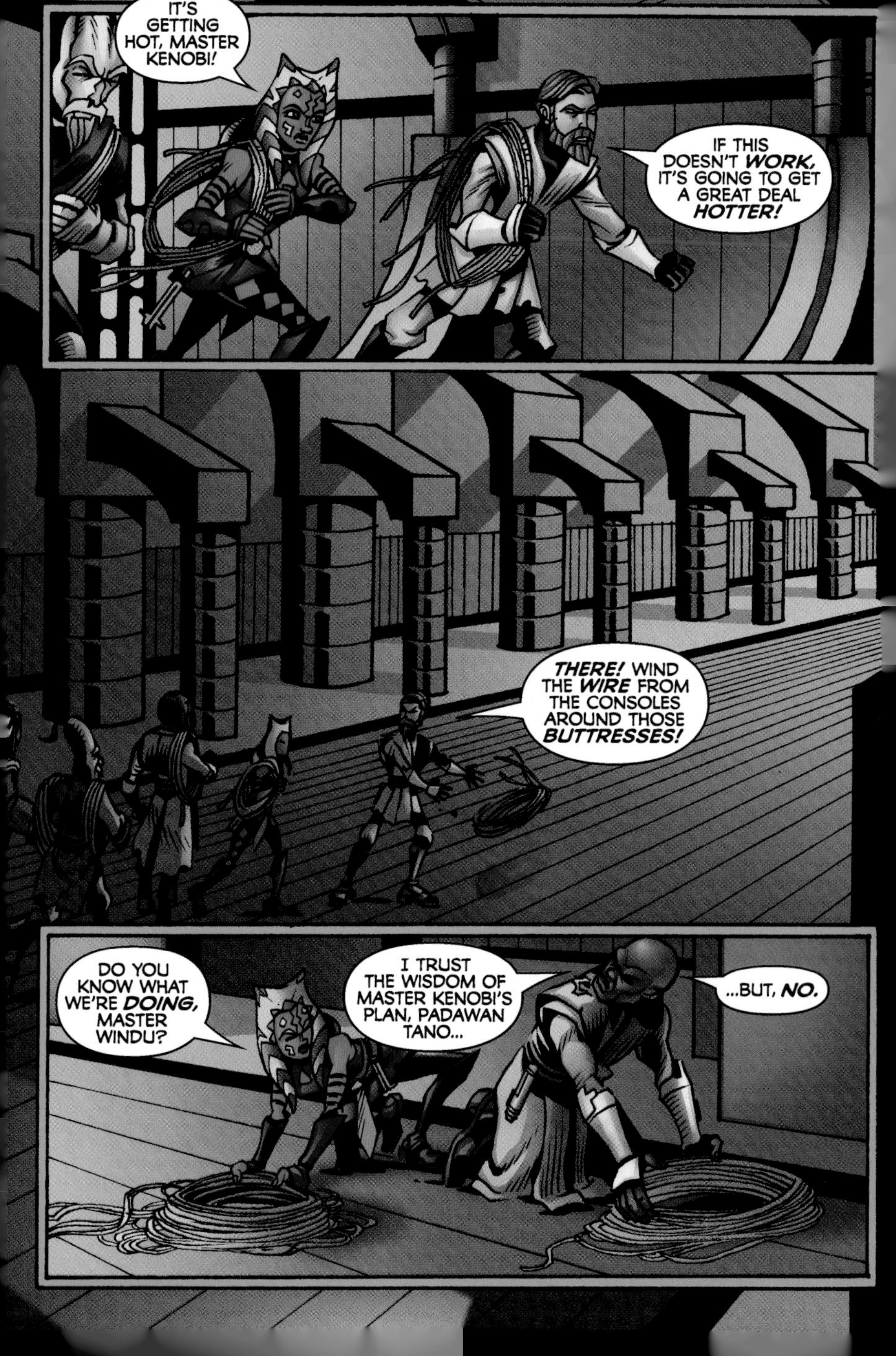
IT'S GETTING HOT, MASTER KENOBI!
IF THIS DOESN'T WORK, IT'S GOING TO GET A GREAT DEAL HOTTER!
THERE! WIND THE WIRE FROM THE CONSOLES AROUND THOSE BUTTRESSES!
DO YOU KNOW WHAT WE'RE DOING, MASTER WINDU?
I TRUST THE WISDOM OF MASTER KENOBI'S PLAN, PADAWAN TANO...
...BUT, NO.

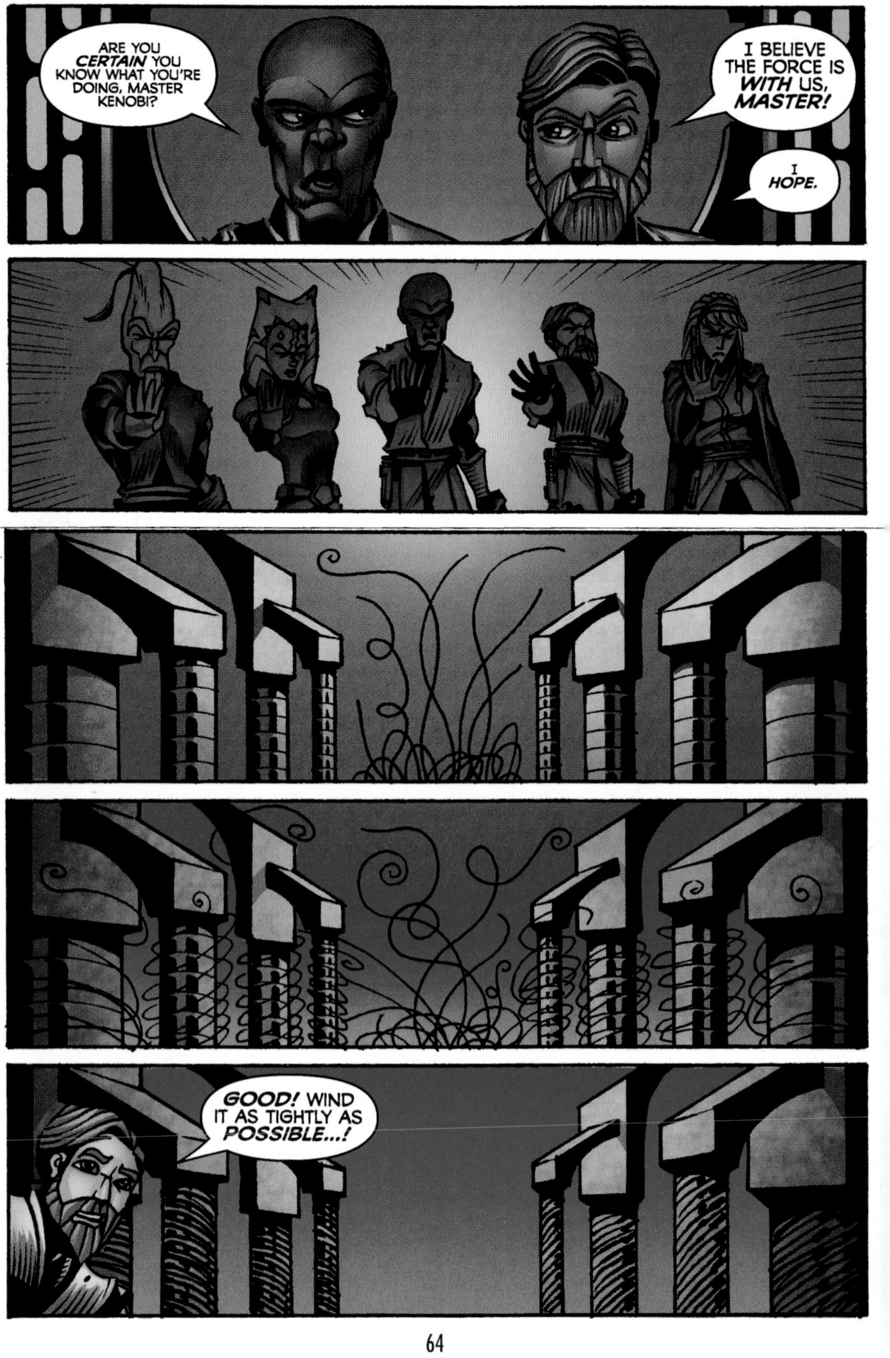
ARE YOU *CERTAIN* YOU KNOW WHAT YOU'RE DOING, MASTER KENOBI?
I BELIEVE THE FORCE IS *WITH* US, *MASTER!*
I *HOPE.*
GOOD! WIND IT AS TIGHTLY AS *POSSIBLE...!*

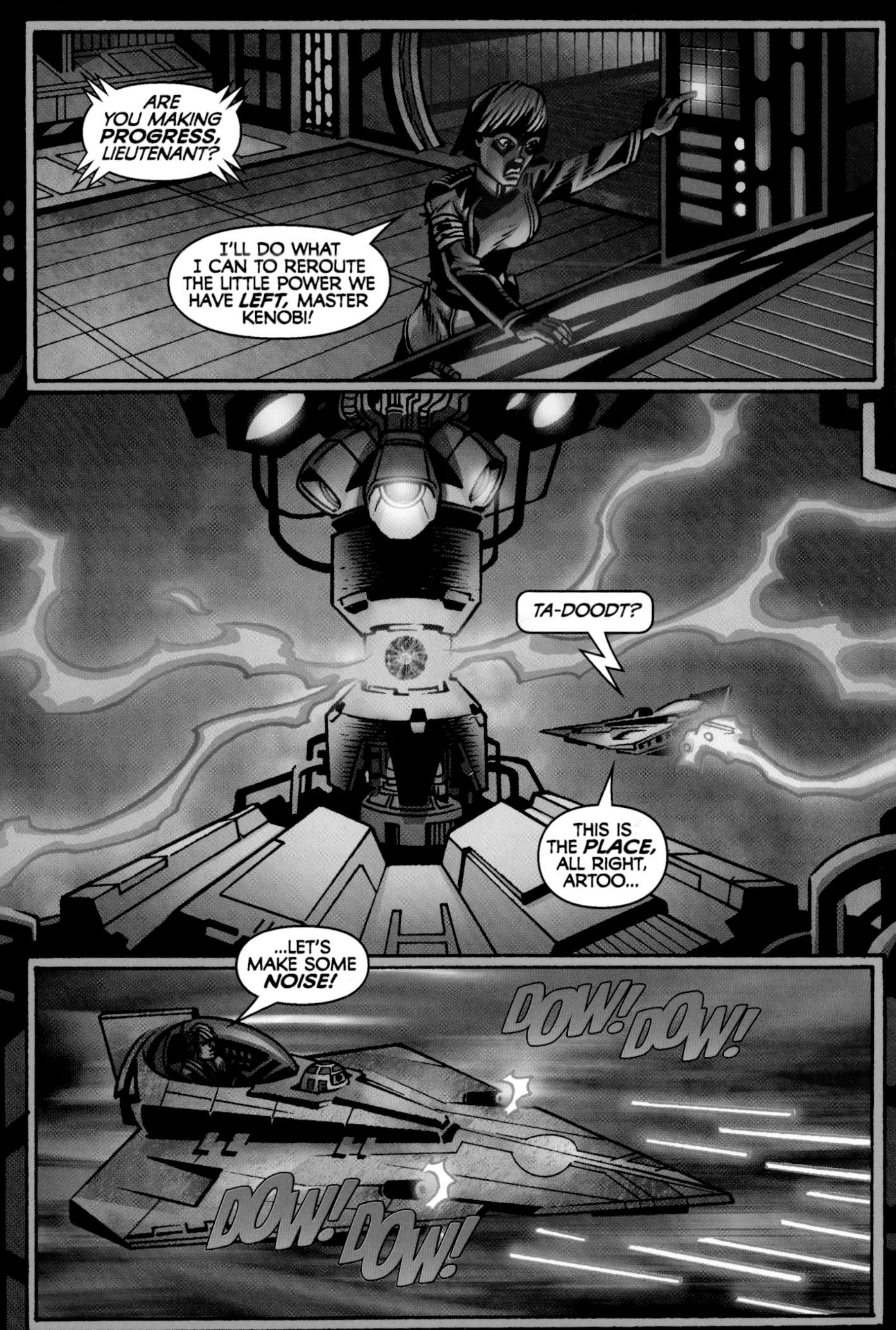
ARE YOU MAKING PROGRESS, LIEUTENANT?
I'LL DO WHAT I CAN TO REROUTE THE LITTLE POWER WE HAVE LEFT, MASTER KENOBI!
TA-DOODT?
THIS IS THE PLACE, ALL RIGHT, ARTOO...
...LET'S MAKE SOME NOISE!
DOW! DOW!
DOW! DOW!

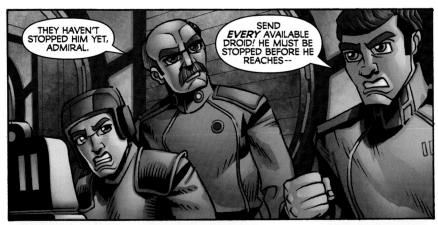

THEY HAVEN'T STOPPED HIM YET, ADMIRAL.

SEND *EVERY* AVAILABLE DROID! HE MUST BE STOPPED BEFORE HE REACHES--

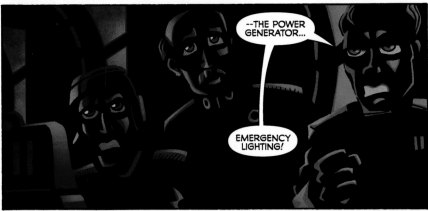

--THE POWER GENERATOR...

EMERGENCY LIGHTING!

MISSION ACCOMPLISHED, MASTER!

GOOD JOB, ANAKIN! NOW GET *OUT* OF THERE, AS QUICKLY AS POSSIBLE!

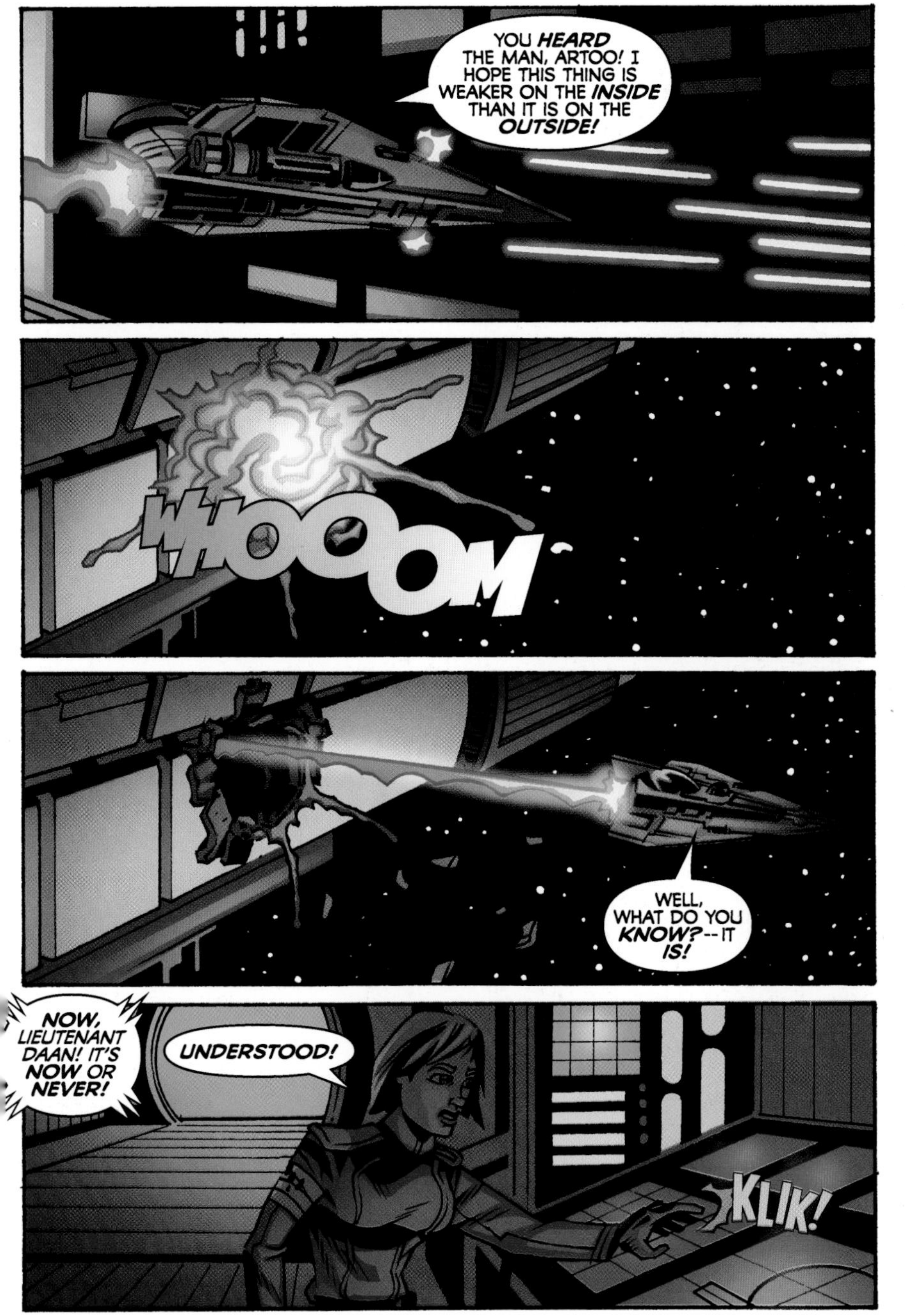
YOU HEARD THE MAN, ARTOO! I HOPE THIS THING IS WEAKER ON THE INSIDE THAN IT IS ON THE OUTSIDE!
WHOOOOM
WELL, WHAT DO YOU KNOW?-- IT IS!
NOW, LIEUTENANT DAAN! IT'S NOW OR NEVER!
UNDERSTOOD!
KLIK!

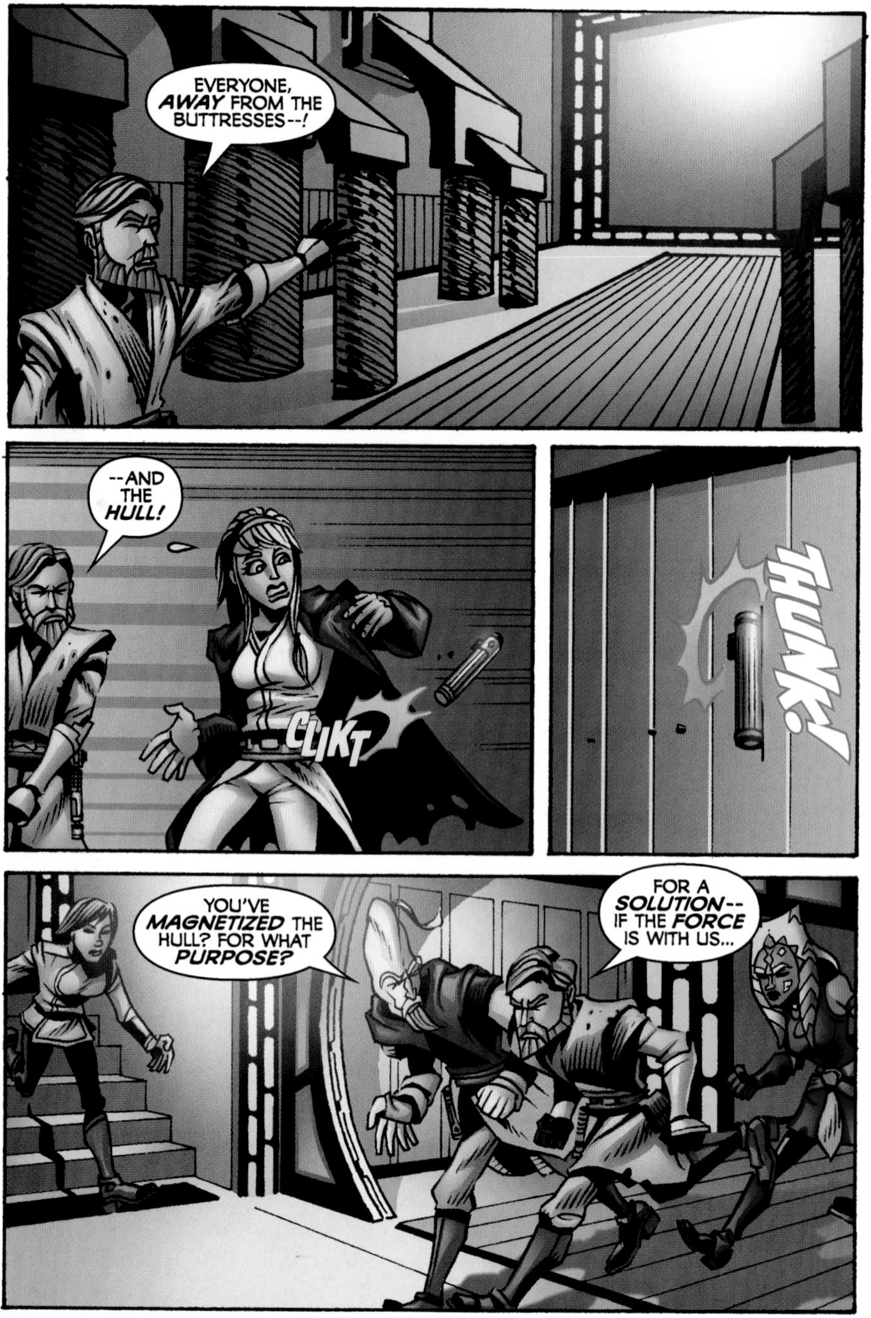
EVERYONE, AWAY FROM THE BUTTRESSES--!
--AND THE HULL!
CLIKT
THUNK!
YOU'VE MAGNETIZED THE HULL? FOR WHAT PURPOSE?
FOR A SOLUTION-- IF THE FORCE IS WITH US...

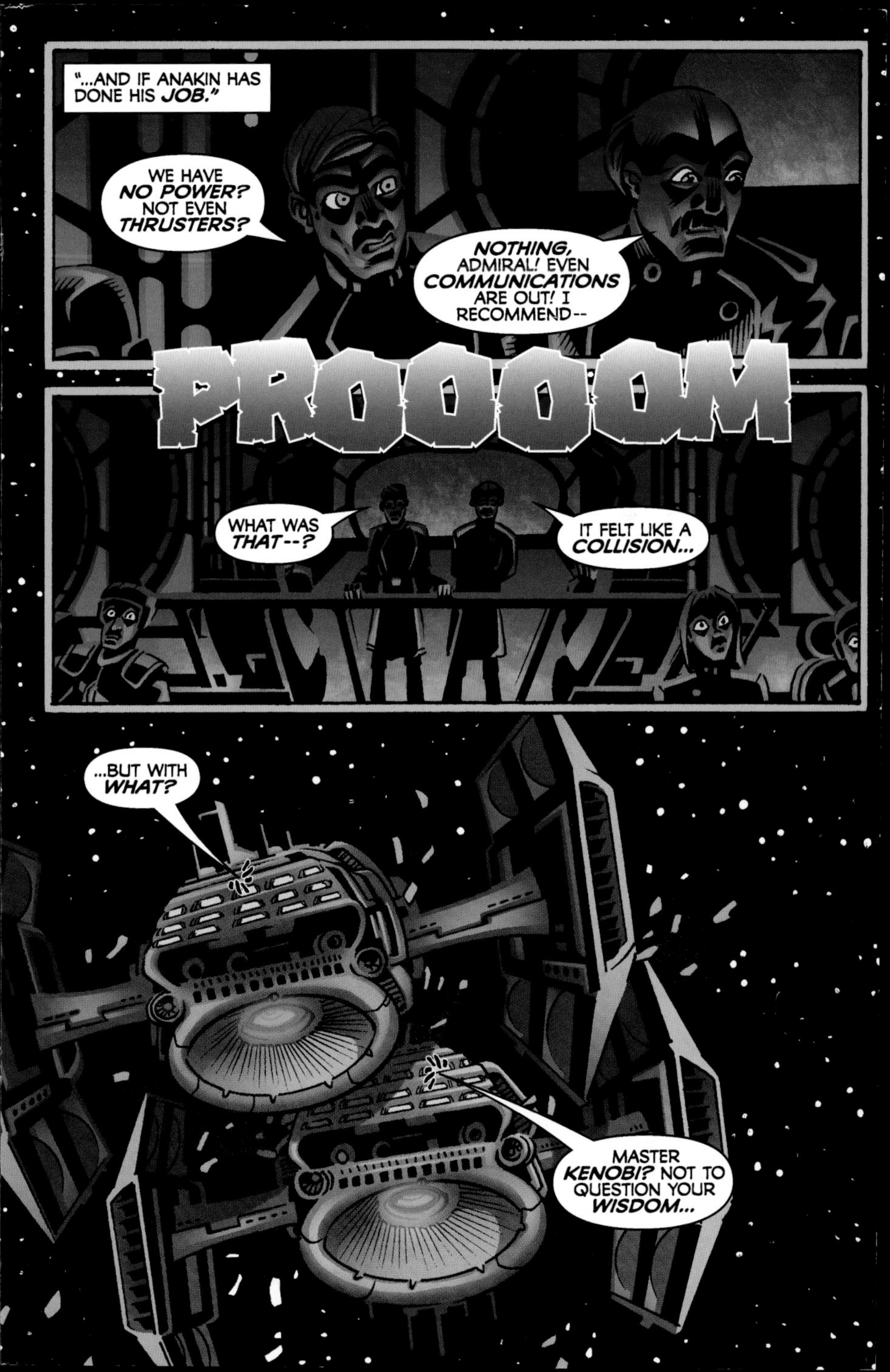

"...AND IF ANAKIN HAS DONE HIS JOB."
WE HAVE NO POWER? NOT EVEN THRUSTERS?
NOTHING, ADMIRAL! EVEN COMMUNICATIONS ARE OUT! I RECOMMEND--
PROOOOM
WHAT WAS THAT--?
IT FELT LIKE A COLLISION...
...BUT WITH WHAT?
MASTER KENOBI? NOT TO QUESTION YOUR WISDOM...

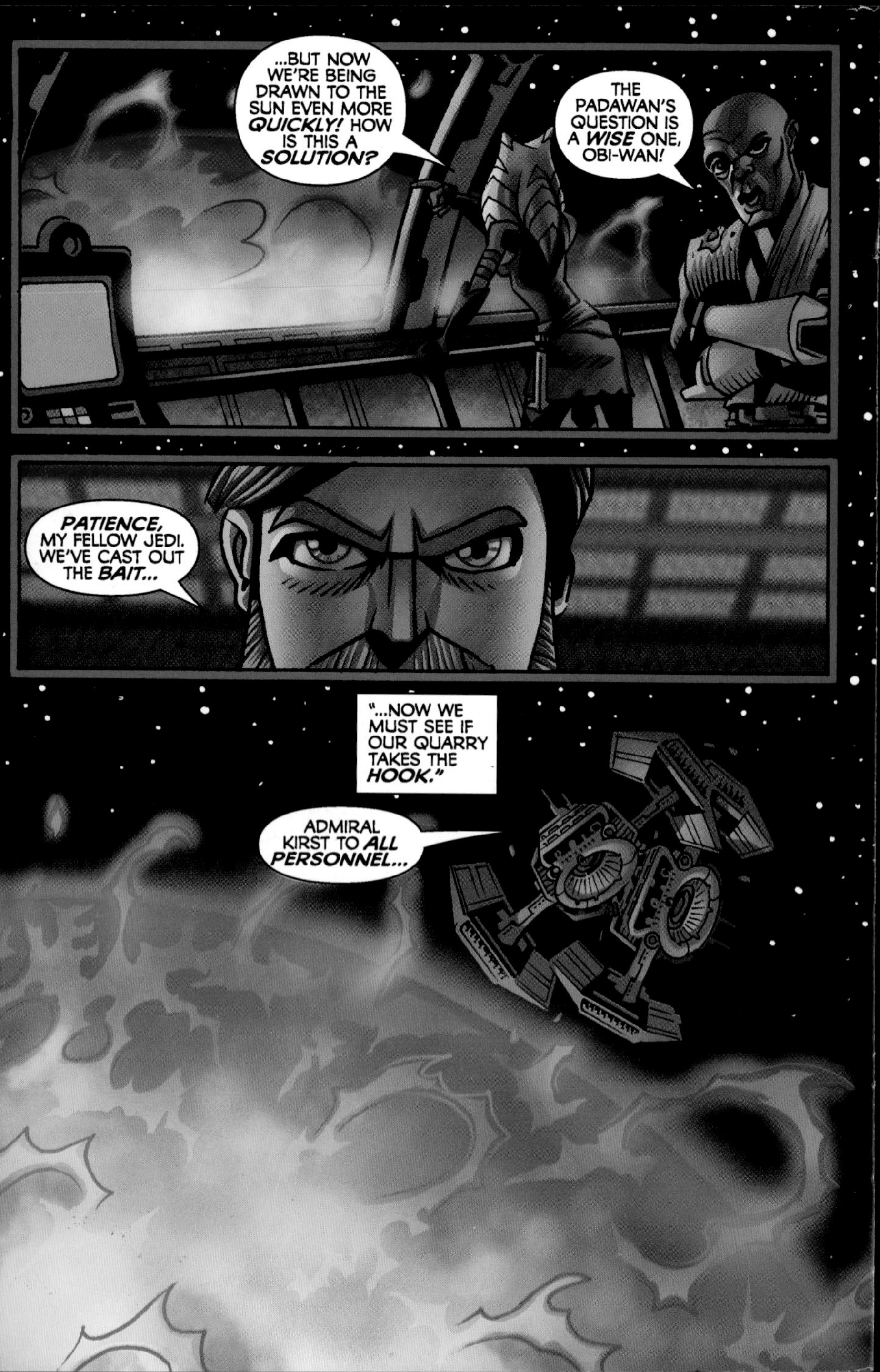
...BUT NOW WE'RE BEING DRAWN TO THE SUN EVEN MORE QUICKLY! HOW IS THIS A SOLUTION?
THE PADAWAN'S QUESTION IS A WISE ONE, OBI-WAN!
PATIENCE, MY FELLOW JEDI. WE'VE CAST OUT THE BAIT...
"...NOW WE MUST SEE IF OUR QUARRY TAKES THE HOOK."
ADMIRAL KIRST TO ALL PERSONNEL...

...REPORT TO YOUR ASSIGNED **ESCAPE PODS** IMMEDIATELY! THIS **IS NOT A DRILL!**

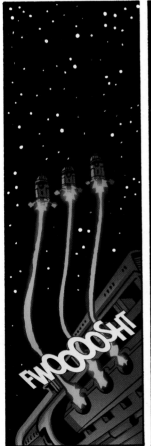

FWOOOOSHT

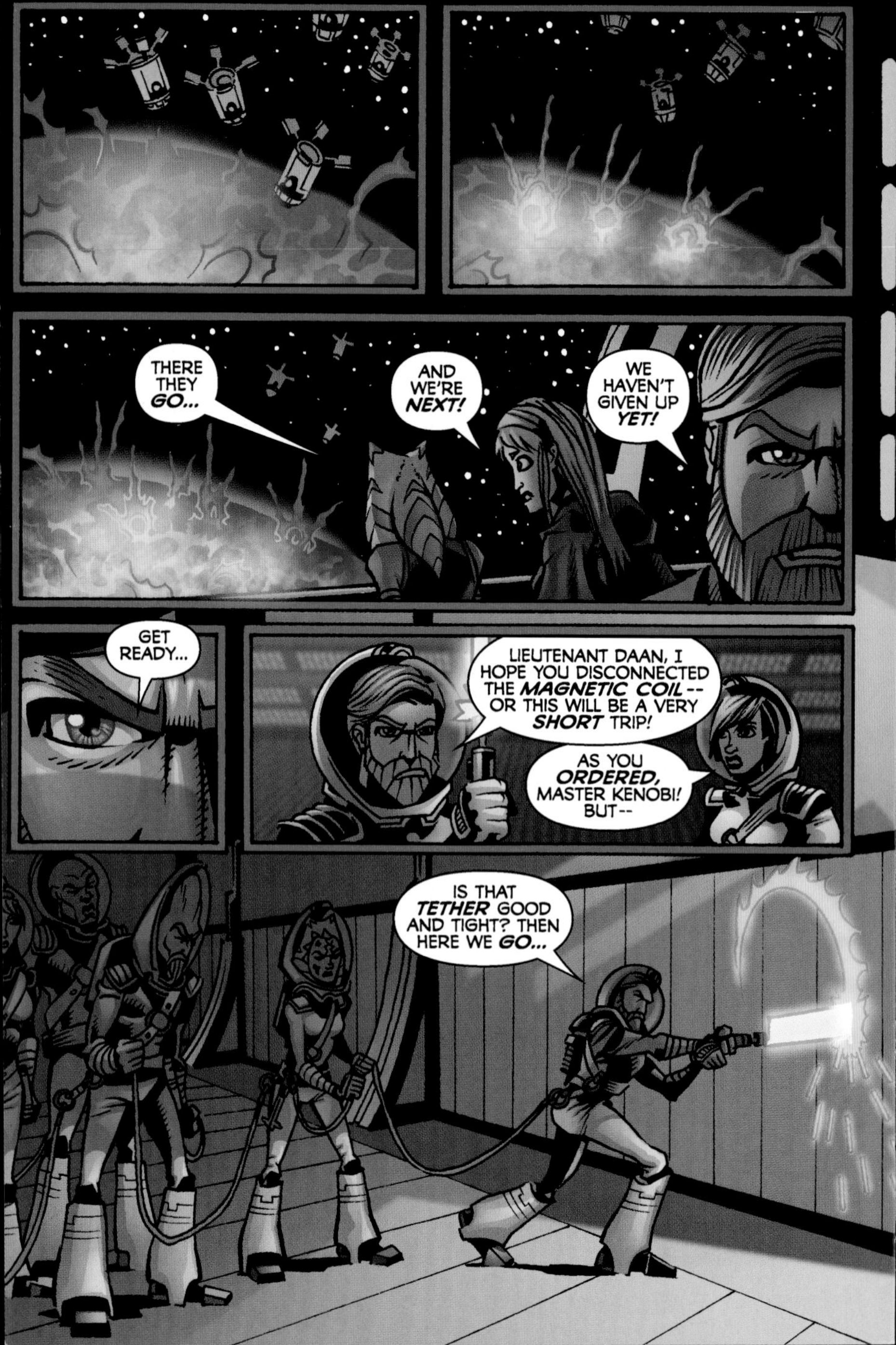
THERE THEY GO...
AND WE'RE NEXT!
WE HAVEN'T GIVEN UP YET!
GET READY...
LIEUTENANT DAAN, I HOPE YOU DISCONNECTED THE MAGNETIC COIL-- OR THIS WILL BE A VERY SHORT TRIP!
AS YOU ORDERED, MASTER KENOBI! BUT--
IS THAT TETHER GOOD AND TIGHT? THEN HERE WE GO...

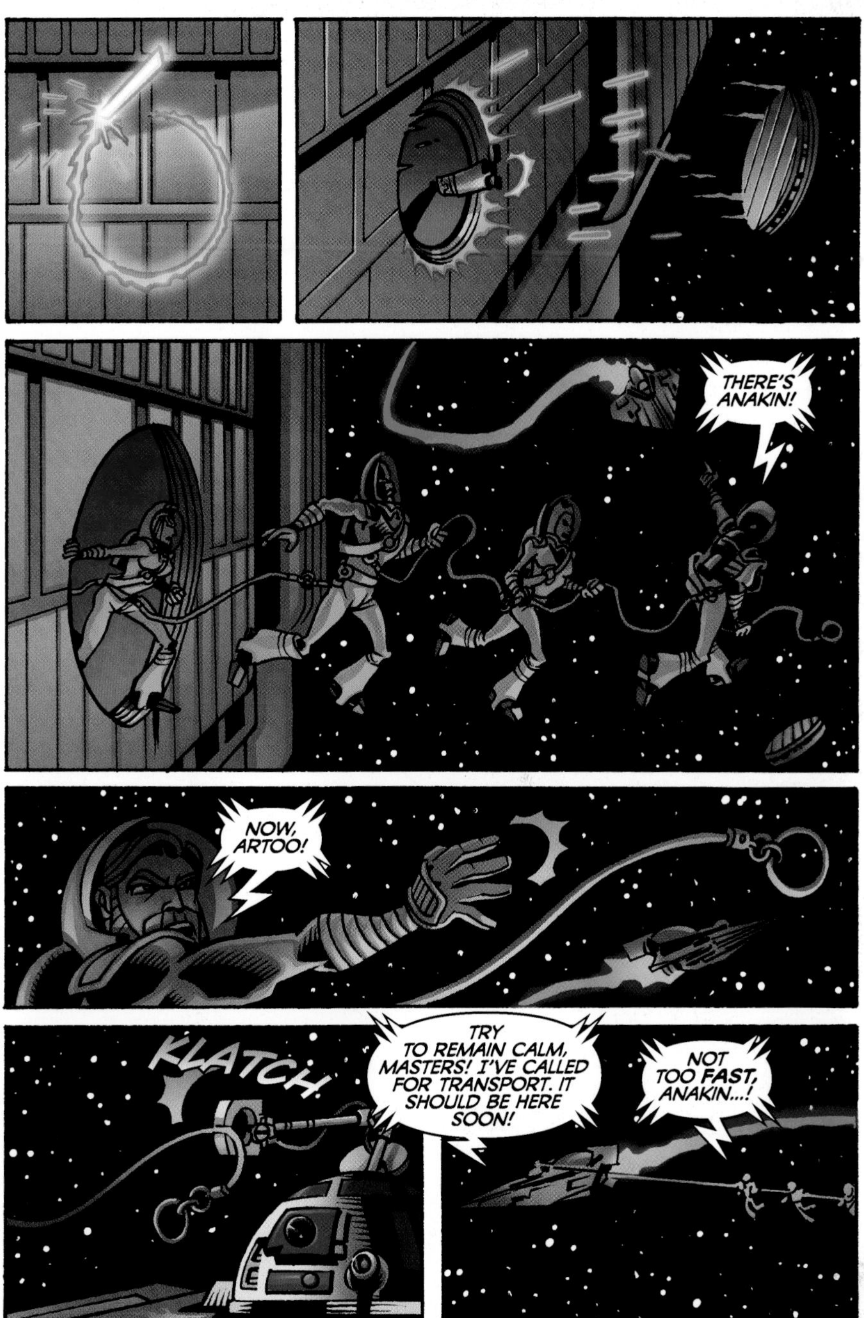
THERE'S ANAKIN!
NOW, ARTOO!
KLATCH
TRY TO REMAIN CALM, MASTERS! I'VE CALLED FOR TRANSPORT. IT SHOULD BE HERE SOON!
NOT TOO FAST, ANAKIN...!

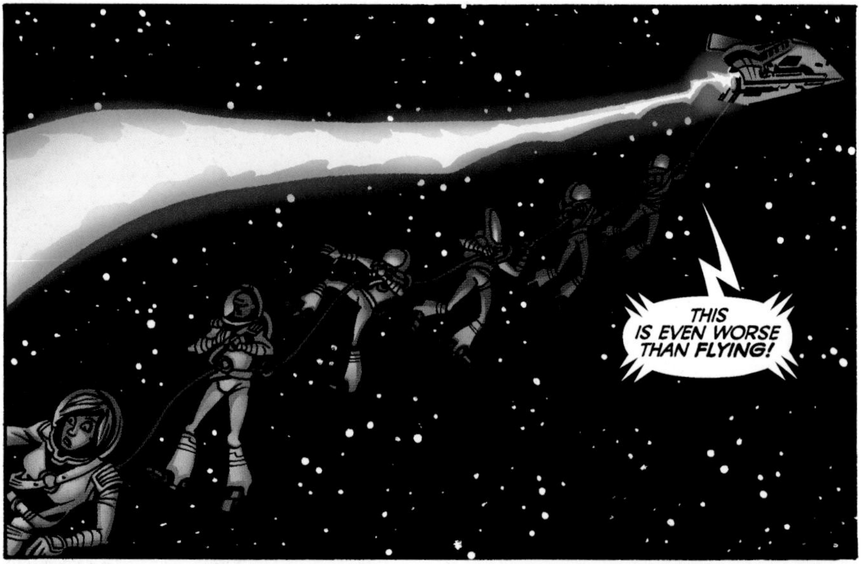
THIS IS EVEN WORSE THAN FLYING!

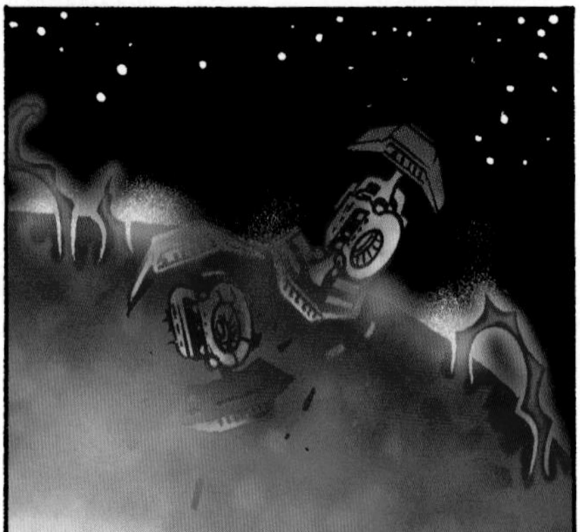

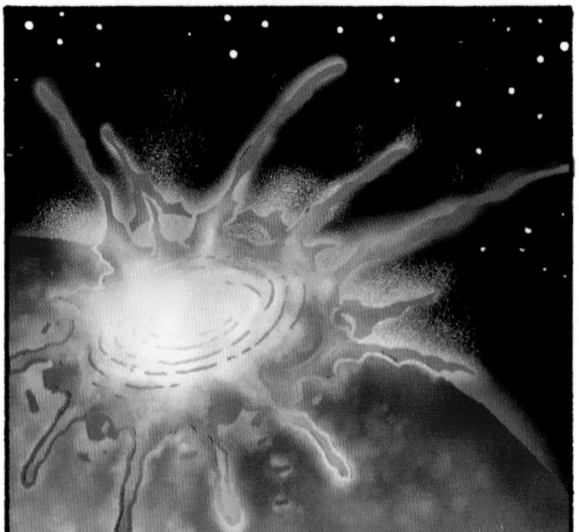

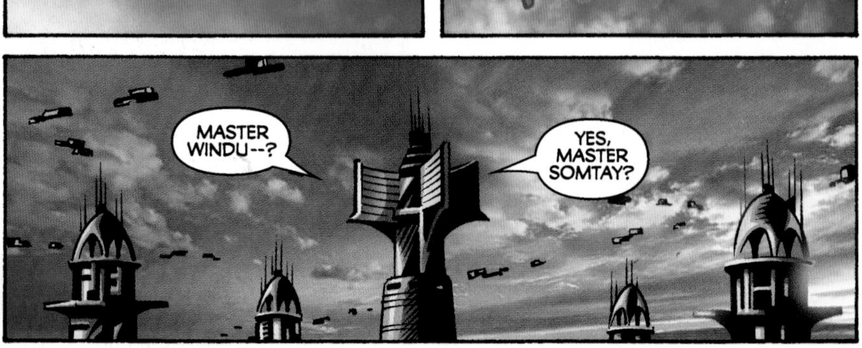
MASTER WINDU--?
YES, MASTER SOMTAY?

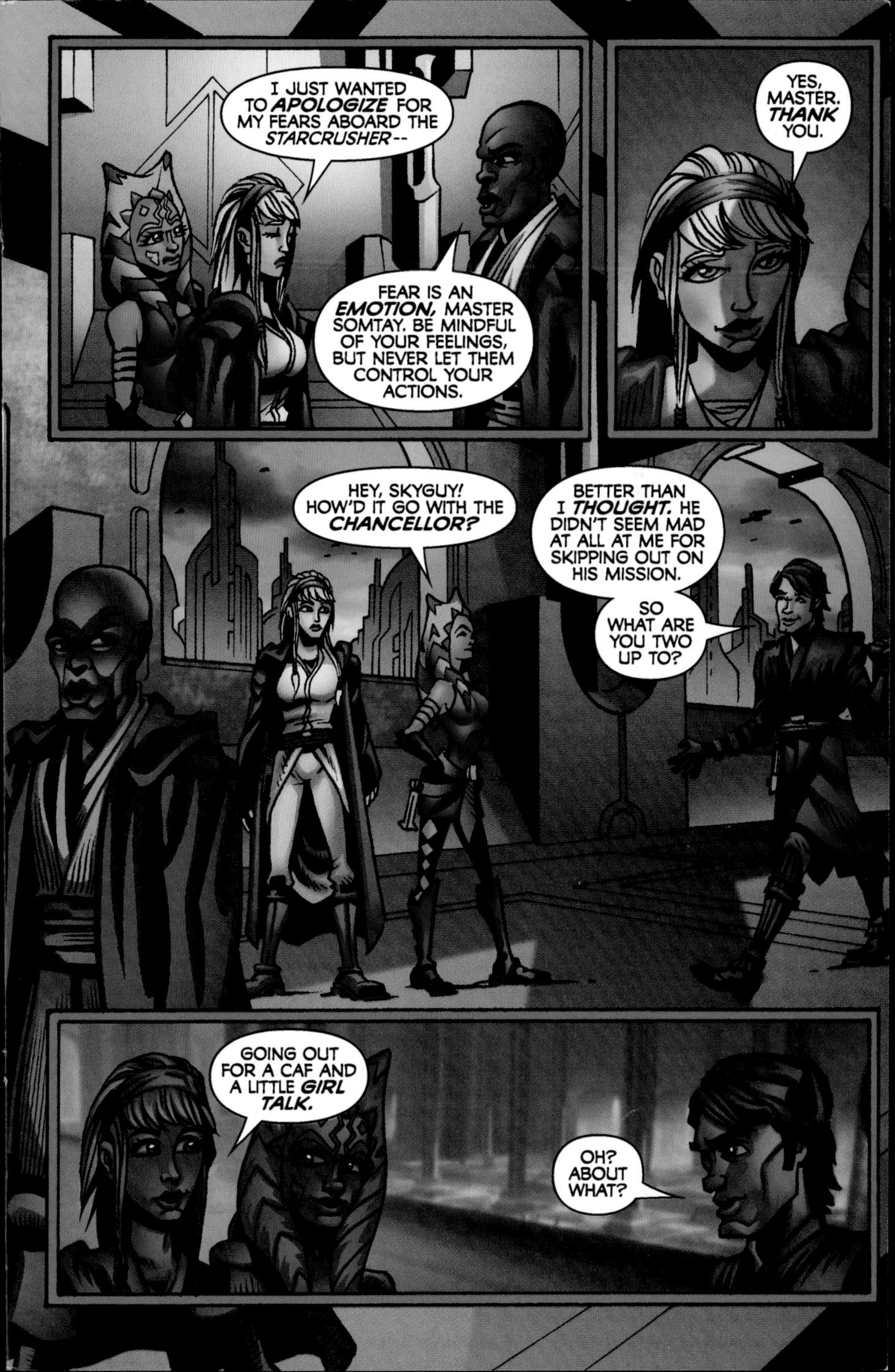
I JUST WANTED TO APOLOGIZE FOR MY FEARS ABOARD THE STARCRUSHER--
FEAR IS AN EMOTION, MASTER SOMTAY. BE MINDFUL OF YOUR FEELINGS, BUT NEVER LET THEM CONTROL YOUR ACTIONS.
YES, MASTER. THANK YOU.
HEY, SKYGUY! HOW'D IT GO WITH THE CHANCELLOR?
BETTER THAN I THOUGHT. HE DIDN'T SEEM MAD AT ALL AT ME FOR SKIPPING OUT ON HIS MISSION.
SO WHAT ARE YOU TWO UP TO?
GOING OUT FOR A CAF AND A LITTLE GIRL TALK.
OH? ABOUT WHAT?

ABOUT *YOU*... MASTER!

WHAT I WOULDN'T GIVE TO BE A ZESS-FLY ON THE WALL FOR *THAT* CONVERSATION!

THE *JEDI* HAVE **WON** THIS TIME. THEY HAVE WON AGAIN.

BUT HIS PATIENCE IS AS INFINITE AS THE **FORCE**. HE HAS **OTHER** SCHEMES...

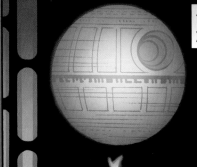

...HIS VICTORY WILL BE ALL THE **SWEETER** FOR ITS LONG DELAY.

THE END

®

PRESIDENT AND PUBLISHER **MIKE RICHARDSON**

EXECUTIVE VICE PRESIDENT **NEIL HANKERSON**

CHIEF FINANCIAL OFFICER **TOM WEDDLE**

VICE PRESIDENT OF PUBLISHING **RANDY STRADLEY**

VICE PRESIDENT OF BOOK TRADE SALES **MICHAEL MARTENS**

VICE PRESIDENT OF BUSINESS AFFAIRS **ANITA NELSON**

VICE PRESIDENT OF MARKETING **MICHA HERSHMAN**

VICE PRESIDENT OF PRODUCT DEVELOPMENT **DAVID SCROGGY**

VICE PRESIDENT OF INFORMATION TECHNOLOGY **DALE LAFOUNTAIN**

SENIOR DIRECTOR OF PRINT, DESIGN, AND PRODUCTION **DARLENE VOGEL**

GENERAL COUNSEL **KEN LIZZI**

EDITORIAL DIRECTOR **DAVEY ESTRADA**

SENIOR MANAGING EDITOR **SCOTT ALLIE**

SENIOR BOOKS EDITOR **CHRIS WARNER**

EXECUTIVE EDITOR **DIANA SCHUTZ**

DIRECTOR OF PRINT AND DEVELOPMENT **CARY GRAZZINI**

ART DIRECTOR **LIA RIBACCHI**

DIRECTOR OF SCHEDULING **CARA NIECE**

STAR WARS GRAPHIC NOVEL TIMELINE (IN YEARS)

Omnibus: Tales of the Jedi—5,000–3,986 BSW4
Knights of the Old Republic—3,964–3,963 BSW4
The Old Republic—3653, 3678 BSW4
Knight Errant—1,032 BSW4
Jedi vs. Sith—1,000 BSW4
Omnibus: Rise of the Sith—33 BSW4
Episode I: The Phantom Menace—32 BSW4
Omnibus: Emissaries and Assassins—32 BSW4
Twilight—31 BSW4
Omnibus: Menace Revealed—31–22 BSW4
Darkness—30 BSW4
The Stark Hyperspace War—30 BSW4
Rite of Passage—28 BSW4
Honor and Duty—22 BSW4
Blood Ties—22 BSW4
Episode II: Attack of the Clones—22 BSW4
Clone Wars—22–19 BSW4
Clone Wars Adventures—22–19 BSW4
General Grievous—22–19 BSW4
Episode III: Revenge of the Sith—19 BSW4
Dark Times—19 BSW4
Omnibus: Droids—5.5 BSW4
Boba Fett: Enemy of the Empire—3 BSW4
Underworld—1 BSW4
Episode IV: A New Hope—SW4
Classic Star Wars—0–3 ASW4
A Long Time Ago . . . —0–4 ASW4
Empire—0 ASW4
Rebellion—0 ASW4
Boba Fett: Man with a Mission—0 ASW4
Omnibus: Early Victories—0–3 ASW4
Jabba the Hutt: The Art of the Deal—1 ASW4
Episode V: The Empire Strikes Back—3 ASW4
Omnibus: Shadows of the Empire—3.5–4.5 ASW4
Episode VI: Return of the Jedi—4 ASW4
Omnibus: X-Wing Rogue Squadron—4–5 ASW4
Heir to the Empire—9 ASW4
Dark Force Rising—9 ASW4
The Last Command—9 ASW4
Dark Empire—10 ASW4
Boba Fett: Death, Lies, and Treachery—10 ASW4
Crimson Empire—11 ASW4
Jedi Academy: Leviathan—12 ASW4
Union—19 ASW4
Chewbacca—25 ASW4
Invasion—25 ASW4
Legacy—130–137 ASW4

Old Republic Era
25,000 – 1000 years before
Star Wars: A New Hope

Rise of the Empire Era
1000 – 0 years before
Star Wars: A New Hope

Rebellion Era
0 – 5 years after
Star Wars: A New Hope

New Republic Era
5 – 25 years after
Star Wars: A New Hope

New Jedi Order Era
25+ years after
Star Wars: A New Hope

Legacy Era
130+ years after
Star Wars: A New Hope

Vector
Crosses four eras in the timeline

Volume 1
Knights of the Old Republic Volume 5
Dark Times Volume 3
Volume 2
Rebellion Volume 4
Legacy Volume 6

BSW4 = before *Episode IV: A New Hope*. ASW4 = after *Episode IV: A New Hope*.

FOR MORE ADVENTURE IN A GALAXY FAR, FAR, AWAY . . .

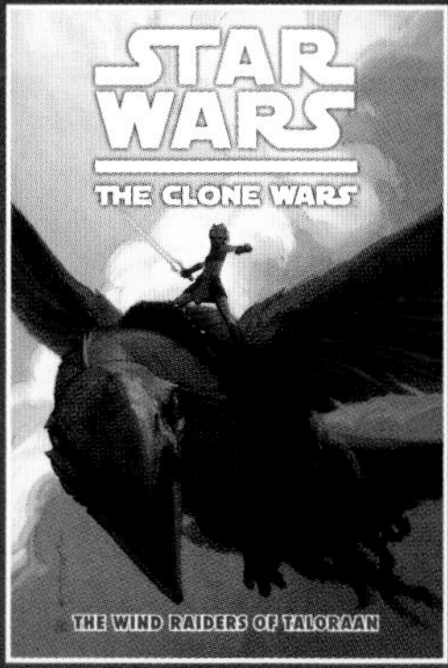
STAR WARS
THE CLONE WARS
THE WIND RAIDERS OF TALORAAN

STAR WARS: THE CLONE WARS—THE WIND RAIDERS OF TALORAAN
978-1-59582-231-4 | $7.99

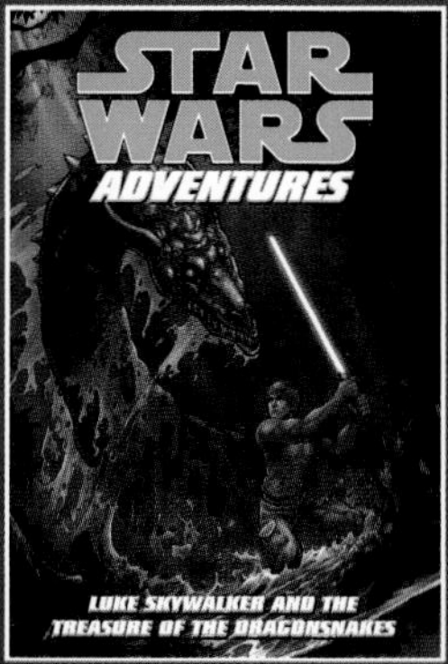
STAR WARS
ADVENTURES
LUKE SKYWALKER AND THE TREASURE OF THE DRAGONSNAKES

STAR WARS ADVENTURES: LUKE SKYWALKER AND THE TREASURE OF THE DRAGONSNAKES
978-1-59582-347-2 | $7.99

STAR WARS ADVENTURES: HAN SOLO AND THE HOLLOW MOON OF KHORYA
978-1-59582-198-0 | $7.99

STAR WARS ADVENTURES: PRINCESS LEIA AND THE ROYAL RANSOM
978-1-59582-147-8 | $7.99

STAR WARS ADVENTURES: THE WILL OF DARTH VADER
978-1-59582-435-6 | $7.99

STAR WARS: THE CLONE WARS—THE COLOSSUS OF DESTINY
978-1-59582-416-5 | $7.99

STAR WARS: THE CLONE WARS—SHIPYARDS OF DOOM
978-1-59582-207-9 | $7.99

STAR WARS: THE CLONE WARS—CRASH COURSE
978-1-59582-230-7 | $7.99

STAR WARS: THE CLONE WARS—SLAVES OF THE REPUBLIC
978-1-59582-349-6 | $9.99

STAR WARS: THE CLONE WARS—IN SERVICE OF THE REPUBLIC
978-1-59582-487-5 | $7.99

STAR WARS: THE CLONE WARS—HERO OF THE CONFEDERACY
978-1-59582-552-0 | $7.99

STAR WARS: THE CLONE WARS—DEADLY HANDS OF SHON-JU
978-1-59582-545-2 | $7.99

DARK HORSE BOOKS
darkhorse.com

AVAILABLE AT YOUR LOCAL COMICS SHOP OR BOOKSTORE

To find a comics shop in your area, call 1-888-266-4226

For more information or to order direct: • On the web: darkhorse.com • E-mail: mailorder@darkhorse.com
Phone: 1-800-862-0052 Mon.–Fri. 9 AM to 5 PM Pacific Time.

STAR WARS ®
CLONE WARS
ADVENTURES

Don't miss any of the action-packed adventures of your favorite **STAR WARS**® characters, available at comics shops and bookstores in a galaxy near you!

$6.99 each!